CREATING CUSTOMERS

An Action Plan for Maximizing Sales, Promotion and Publicity for the Small Business

David H. Bangs , Jr.
and
The Editors of *Common Sense*

Upstart Publishing Company, Inc.
Dover, New Hampshire

Published by Upstart Publishing Company, Inc.
A Division of Dearborn Publishing Group, Inc.
12 Portland Street, Dover, New Hampshire 03820
(800) 235-8866 or (603) 749-5071

Neither the author nor the publisher of this book is engaged in rendering, by the sale of this book, legal, accounting or other professional services. The reader is encouraged to employ the services of a competent professional in such matters.

Library of Congress Catalog Number 90-071900
ISBN: 0-936894-27-X

Book Design by Brad Robeson

Printed in the United States of America.

For a complete catalog of Upstart's small business publications call (800) 235-8866.

Table
of Contents

....

Foreword

Creating Customers is a compilation of articles written to help you manage the most important—and toughest—job in business. You have to have customers. Everything else is ancillary. Staffing, financing, producing, planning, and directing are subordinate to one end: creating customers.

Business boils down to making sales. You don't find customers. You don't stumble across them, or even seek them out. You create customers by taking action. You select target markets and choose products you might sell them, promote your goods and services to make the market aware that you are in business to have what they want, and finally (you hope) make the sale and begin the cycle again.

The success of your business is directly related to how good you and your organization are at this central task. I know. I learned this the hard way, back in 1977 when I started Upstart Publishing. I'd been a banker and a consultant to small businesses for years, so you might think I would know what I was up to. But like many people who start small enterprises my experience was one-sided. In my case it was heavily weighted towards finance, and while I knew that marketing (another way of putting "creating customers") was important, I thought that with good publications and professional advertising support customers would fight to buy my wares.

Wrong. I'd spotted a good market niche: small business owners who wanted to improve their businesses but weren't sure where to start. Small business owners, as a group, are highly motivated and intelligent and tend to be profit and goal-oriented. All the studies said so. Well then, I figured, since I'd been working with small business owners for a number of years, and all of them were interested in improving their businesses (or keeping them afloat), and my experience squared with the opinions of experts, there must be a lot more people like them out there in the market* I'd reach them by direct mail.

Upstart's first publication was *Common Sense*, a series of short how-to articles packaged in a monthly newsletter format. We (by now I'd involved others in the enterprise) hired a professional direct mail company to help us choose lists and put together an enticing package, invested some $15,000 in the promotion, and sent out thousands of packages. We then sat back and waited for the flood of orders.

It never materialized. We received plenty of inquiries for the "bill me" option from people wanting something-for-nothing. Not from real customers. Individual owners of small businesses didn't respond at all. We got a smattering of paid-with-order responses from two other groups, consultants and accountants. That was it. The total return, including those who paid later, was on the order of $2,500.

The lessons I learned from this first foray into direct mail eventually were distilled into a series of *Common Sense* topics written by a nationally known direct mail expert, Roger Parker, who helped me redirect Upstart's efforts. We had to find other ways of creating customers, which led us into working with dozens of banks nationwide ranging in size from Chase Manhattan to the 1st National Bank of Lebanon, NH. These accounts want to help their small business clients succeed and help us by chipping in ideas of what their customer want to know. Many of those individual customers contact us directly with specific questions and suggestions.

As a result, we make sure that every *Common Sense* article from which the chapters of this book are adapted is directed to problems faced by small business owners and provide step-by-step solutions to those problems. We thought (and still do) that if we put a tool into your hands and show you how it's used, you can take it the rest of the way. We (the staff editors and contributors) seek out solutions for you to use, but it is up to you to implement these solutions in a manner that fits your business.

Every chapter in *Creating Customers* is based on real-life experience. Writers whose work appears in *Common Sense* are seasoned business owners or managers who have gone through the marketing mill and learned how to create customers for their own businesses. We purposely avoided articles written by non-practitioners from the start, not because academic and other experts have nothing useful to say, but because we wanted *Common Sense* topics to reflect what actually works in practice. If it's in this book, it works.

---

*Note the error: entrepreneurs seek consulting help only when their problems are unbearable, so this had been a self-selected group in the first place. Generalizing from a small sample often leads to erroneous conclusions. Phooey. I knew better.

Creating Customers is a tool kit. Each chapter will help you with a specific aspect of the marketing process. Some will help you save money, others will sharpen your focus on those individuals who are most likely to become your customers in the future. The cumulative effect is to put Upstart's contributors' experience at your disposal. There's no need to learn how to create customers by blundering around.

Good luck. If you have any thoughts or suggestions on *Creating Customers* or any other aspect of running a small enterprise, please write or call me. Upstart is always looking for good ideas, including corrections to and improvements of our books and newsletters.

David H. "Andy" Bangs Jr., Editor

Portsmouth, New Hampshire

Chapter One:

The Four Stages of Strategic Planning

··

The process of strategic planning is an end in itself. From the process you will gain a different way of looking at your business and its prospects—and that different viewpoint will result in increased sales, new products, new markets, and heightened profitability.

The strategic plan itself is a written document outlining the steps—including checkpoints and schedules—needed to get from where your business is now to where you want it to be in five or more years. As the process of planning unfolds, you will find that you have to examine your assumptions about the nature of your business, products, markets, and operations. This cannot be rushed. As you proceed, you will want to modify the plan as circumstances seem to demand. But keep changes to a minimum. You will almost surely find what other business owners have found: A steady course is better than one which changes with every shift in the wind.

In very large businesses, strategic planning usually involves four stages: financial planning (to establish budgets), forecasting (multi-year financial planning), qualitative planning (shifting to a new market or to new regulations), and finally to a stage where strategic planning is so integral that it is part of daily management thinking.

You have an advantage here. A smaller business—whether doing a quarter of a million dollars or twenty million—can take advantage of its competitors' lack of planning (strategic or otherwise), while almost every large business plans strategically.

Who needs strategic planning? Every business owner or manager who wants his or her business to remain profitable and grow.

What can you expect to get out of the strategic planning process? A new way of looking at your strategic options. A competitive edge. Greater control over the future of your business. A valuable addition to your normal business planning efforts, one where you can systematically exploit market gaps and niches.

The cost? An effective strategic plan can be written in a weekend. The data-gathering time may be longer, but much of the information is probably available to you already. The market analysis may take longer—but any time you spend examining current and future markets is time well spent. (Even if you don't plan strategically in a formal way, you will find that your business has a strategy.)

The cost is minimal. The benefits are sizable. Once you start, the process is not difficult and can be exciting.

You may want to involve your colleagues and employees in the process. This will have a number of positive effects. Employees have good ideas of how to work more productively, how to solve internal problems that can get in the way of growth, and even what kind of products the market may want in the future. If they are kept involved, their input will be considerable. If major changes in operations result from the planning process, your employees won't resist as they might otherwise.

Figure 1.1

Goals

Strategic planning must define qualitative goals. These qualitative goals will include:

Positioning: What is the position of your organization in its marketplace and among its competitors?

Segmentation: What are the demographics and qualitative characteristics (attitudes and tastes) of the defined market segment?

Cultural: How is the "culture" of your organization defined?

Stylistic: What is the style of your organization?

Differentiation: In what ways does your organization and its product/service structure differ from all other organizations offering similar products and services?

Functional: What purpose does your organization and its product/service structure fulfill beyond its own needs?

Quantitative: What quantitative elements must be defined? These will include price strategy, market share, growth rate, cost characteristics, and production/distribution logistics.

All strategic elements must be defined in terms of needs, attitudes, and unmet desires in the market. These will include known needs that can be accurately determined by investigations, and hypothetical needs that must be nourished to become a market need.

You should involve your banker, your accountant, and possibly your other professional advisors. Even if they don't agree with the strategies you propose, their advice at the planning stage will present options you may not think of yourself.

Finally, you may find that you could benefit from the help of professional strategic planners. Their cost is trivial compared with potential benefits—a poorly thought out expansion avoided, a new opportunity seized, the right new product for existing customers.

The process begins with looking at the marketplace.

Examine the business arena

The purpose of this first step is to focus on the external environment in which your business operates.

Your marketplace is full of competition. Most obvious are your direct competitors, those businesses which sell the same kind of products to the same markets you do—at the same prices. But you also need to identify indirect competitors—those businesses which might compete with yours in some way.

If you do nothing more than find out who your competition is, what their strengths and weaknesses are, and apply those insights to your business, you'll seize an advantage. Most business owners fail to closely examine the competition—and often overlook the potential competition altogether, even if they do manage to identify the most direct competitors.

One useful thing about looking at your competitors is that it helps you define your own business, not in terms of what you are currently selling or producing but in terms of the marketplace. Don't bother to make an exhaustive analysis of the competition at this point, though. Ask yourself the questions in Figure 1.2, jot down the answers, and concentrate on answering the question "What business am I in?" Do you see the need for your business's products or services increasing in the near future? Decreasing? Is the market expanding or will you have to seek out other markets? (See figure 1.3)

The primary aim of creating a set of workable strategies for your business is to guarantee continued profitability and growth. That's tough if your market is growing less rapidly than the buggy whip industry, yet many businesses doom themselves to

---

Figure 1.2

The Competition

☐ Who are your five most important competitors?

☐ What other companies (or industries) could become forces in your market within in the next five years?

☐ How do you stack up against your competitors—are you on the weak or dominant end of the continuum?

☐ What are you going to do about it?

Figure 1.3

What Business Am I In?

Product definition: What products do we make?

Technology definition: What technologies are we competent in?

Market definition: What markets do we currently sell to? Could we sell to in the future? Would we like to sell to?

Conceptual definition: If the person next to me in an airplane asked what makes our business unique, what would I say? Can I express our corporate philosophy in a short sentence?

These are all ways to answer the question: What business am I in? A comprehensive answer would include aspects of each of the four definitions.

---

failure by forgetting that the market is always changing. Baldwin Locomotive made wonderful steam engines, but their market evaporated.

This step can help you focus on the potential markets your company could pursue. If you can position yourself to take advantage of inevitable changes, you will have discovered your most effective strategy.

This requires that you know what business you are in now, and what strengths and weaknesses your competition has. It also requires that you begin to think about what you want your business to be in five or ten years.

Look outside the business. What is the business environment like? What do you think the economy will be like in the next several years? Will your business be affected by any political changes you see as possible?

Let your mind roam over these kinds of questions for a few minutes, then fill in Figure 1.4 on the next page.

Examine internal operations

Once you've looked outside the business you can then look within, at the internal operations which you have more control over.

As the strategic planning process continues, you should find two things happening. First, you will find that many things you may have been viewing as beyond control become at least partially controllable. Second, as you review the internal operations of your business and begin to gather information from your employees about how they would improve operations, productivity and profitability begin to rise. These two series of events are closely related. As efficiency improves, so does control over forces once viewed as external. And as the business environment becomes less daunting, more of your efforts will be released for other matters—such as developing new products, new methods of running the business, and better use of resources.

Figure 1.4

Business Definition Worksheet

1. My five closest competitors are:

   _____

2. Possible competition could come from (companies, technologies, industries):

   _____

3. Demand for my products/services is increasing/decreasing:

   _____

4. Products I might discontinue are:

   _____

5. Products I might begin are:

   _____

6. Markets I might enter are:

   _____

7. Markets I might leave are:

   _____

8. My company is unique because:

   _____

9. Right now my company's biggest marketing obstacle is:

   _____

10. Our biggest marketing opportunity is:

    _____

Four areas of internal operations need your close attention. Do not aim for perfection. You can revel in detail later; the first thing to do is to get the framework firm.

If you haven't performed a management audit recently, fill in Figure 1.5. Once you have a rough grasp of strengths and weaknesses in these four critical areas, you can begin to think about what to do about them. Follow the rule of building on strengths and shoring up weaknesses.

All you need to begin with is a list. Discuss this list with colleagues and subordinates to create a starting point for improvement.

In your business plan, you make financial projections (cash flow, profit and loss, perhaps a pro forma balance sheet) based on assumptions about how your business will fare over the next year or so. The projections become operating and capital budgets. These in turn are used to control the use of money in your business.

Figure 1.5

List your strengths and weaknesses in the following areas

Financial _____

_____

_____

Marketing _____

_____

_____

Production/Distribution _____

_____

_____

Personnel development _____

_____

_____

Equally important—if not more important—are projections for marketing, production/distribution, and personnel development. (Granted, you must control cash if you plan to manage at all.)

You have to look pretty far ahead, though, to form reasonable strategies. What markets will you be in? With what products, distribution, finance—and with what people?

A strategic plan will enable you to make the best use (in the sense of most rational, or profitable, or safest) of your resources to reach objective, measurable goals. This step helps establish the starting points: this much capital, these markets, those products, these people with these skills.

As a rule, small- and mid-sized companies tend to have stronger production and marketing skills than financial or personnel development. There's nothing wrong with this; production and marketing skills are what make a business move. Financial and personnel skills, though, are needed to keep it moving. You want to establish a balance among these.

Some financial skills often lacking are the ability to write and live with realistic budgets, having enough capital to meet liquidity needs, managing cash flow, managing credit and collection, and raising capital. If your business always has enough money, good credit, positive cash flow, and no bad debt, chances are it is being run by financial geniuses or penny-pinchers. Or financial conservatives who may be pinching off growth.

Some personnel development warning signs: personnel turnover, old hands promoted beyond their abilities (also known as the Peter Principle), new employees turning out not to have the skills they claimed, excessive absences, tardiness, and waste.

These have standard solutions—of which entrepreneurs tend to be ignorant. When was the last time you heard of a personnel director starting a business? It rarely happens.

Marketing and production problems tend to stick out: missed marketing opportunities, stagnant or sinking sales, returns, slow shipments, quality control problems.

Now go back to Figure 1.5. You may want to recast your answers.

Making lists won't solve any problems. It won't increase sales or put dollars on the bottom line. But it will help you reorganize your strategic thinking—so stick with it.

List your personal goals as they relate to your business

This is a particularly important step. Large publicly held businesses tend to have a life all their own, where the outside directors, representing the investors, keep the business headed in a more or less sensible direction.

Small or privately held businesses are a bit different. The whims of the owners exert a far greater impact on the business strategy than may at first be apparent.

What do you want to get out of your business? What size business do you want to run? What do you hope to be doing in the next five years? What personally difficult decisions have you been putting off? These four questions must be answered comprehensively.

For example, if you want to retire in a few years with a reasonable income, manage nothing more arduous than your garden, and have a buyer waiting to put you on a lifetime consulting contract, your strategic choices are made. If you aren't sure of what you want from a business, you have a different problem, and the personal quandary will affect your judgment.

Some possible personal goals are: make a lot of money, create a business for my children to take over some day, provide jobs for my community, build value against retirement, be in the forefront of new technology, be my own boss, and see how big a company I can make. All of these have been cited as motives by business owners; each has profound implications for the way that owner will run his or her business.

The question of size is important. A small business with a handful of employees who are almost family differs considerably from that same business grown to 300 employees. Some people do not want the problems (and opportunities) offered by a mid-sized business, and if you are one of these persons, better think before embarking on a growth strategy. Slow-growth or non-growth strategies may make more sense for you.

Figure 1.6

Personal Goals for Your Business

Financial

_____

_____

_____

Size of business

_____

_____

_____

Business feel

_____

_____

_____

Risk tolerance

_____

_____

_____

Five-year plan

_____

_____

_____

On the other hand, seeing your ideas take shape, seeing them work, and watching your company grow are exciting. If you're one of those people who don't mind taking limited risks, a growth strategy would perhaps be more appropriate. Maybe more risk is involved, but then the rewards will be greater too.

For others, the challenge of doing what people say can't be done is irresistible. If you are in this camp, turn it to your advantage.

The final question is an odd one: What decisions have you postponed? Postponed decisions point to trouble spots. By becoming more aware of what decisions you are trying to duck, you will find that you can avoid a flock of preventable problems or discover new opportunities.

An example of a postponed decision is a partnership where one partner wants immediate income while the other looks to long, slow growth in the value of the business as the surest route to financial freedom. There's nothing wrong with either goal, but if the partners put off discussing the conflict and make decisions about other business matters as if this essential strategic decision has already been made, trouble is inevitable. If they get the conflict out in the open and make the basic decision (to go for immediate income or aim at long-term growth), a lot of secondary decisions become easier.

Many businesses have gone under because of this kind of unresolved strategic decision. Don't join them.

Figure 1.7 **What Is Your Current Strategy?**	Aggressive Defensive	Active Passive	Goal-oriented Opportunistic
Marketing			
Management			
Financial			
Production			
Operational			

Examine current strategies

Every business is run according to a strategy. There's always a guiding set of goals and assumptions that shape the way business is done.

"Trusting to luck" is a strategy. "Responding to outside pressure" is another. "Inertia" and "habit" are two more—maybe the most common of all. "Business as usual" is more than a catchphrase; it represents a way of thinking about doing business that is at odds with strategic planning.

Unfortunately, most businesses are run according to one of these four "strategies." Look at how they operate: without a coherent plan, without measurable, preset goals and checkpoints to make sure that progress is being made, frequently without budgets. A marketing plan? Why bother? Manpower development plans to make sure the business will have the skills it needs? Of course not.

These "strategies" tend to be unconsciously used. More to the point, they are very poor strategies which are thoughtlessly applied and have evolved as a way of doing business rather than as deliberate methods.

Strategies can be active or passive, aggressive or defensive, goal-oriented or opportunistic. These three sets of pairs can help define your current strategy; apply them to each of the following areas and ask which adjective applies out of each pair.

There is nothing normative about these pairs. No one is "better" than the others; some are more useful for your business at this time than the others. Here is how they relate to various facets of your business:

1. Marketing

Active marketing strategies establish marks for the competition to shoot for, forcing them to scramble to keep up. Passive marketing plays follow-the-leader and can be extremely effective. Aggressive marketing strategies aim for greater market share; defensive marketing tends to hold onto current clients. Goal-oriented marketing strategies set specific targets: dollar and/or unit levels, specific market share percentages, number of new customers, and so on. Opportunistic marketing goes for other methods of growth, tends to be short-range, and is ruthlessly effective at some times for some companies.

2. Management

For all of the blather about how to manage, very few businesses, particularly smaller ones, spend much effort upgrading managerial productivity. Most are managed reactively; a problem pops up, is addressed and resolved. Active management tries to prevent the problem. The way management thinks is a most important strategic issue.

Once your business becomes committed to strategic planning as the corporate philosophy, by constantly reexamining marketing strategies, management will become more active, more aggressive and often more flexible, setting goals and achieving them while also acting opportunistically when that strategy makes sense.

3. Financial

Financial strategies range from survival to expansion. This is a major strategic issue: the wrong strategy is apt to be financially disastrous.

Most businesses tend to be aggressive in their financial plans unless the economy is in a shambles. Most financial managers, though, are rightfully conservative and leave a balance which has all parties a bit frazzled. Sometimes caution makes sense. Sometimes it doesn't. This is one place where strategic planning can afford immediate results; it allows you to prepare an array of options for different sets of circumstances. Then you can sit down with the most conservative treasurer and reach realistic financial strategies.

4. Production

More capacity or less? Increase sales or try to increase margins? Aim for greater output? Economies of scale may apply. Lower production in order to gain greater flexibility? These questions are strategic, and how your company addresses them has far-reaching consequences.

Sometimes it pays to pull back. Sometimes getting ready before demand hits is a good move, but if you don't lay out the possible options (a basic strategic move) you can't make a real choice.

5. Operational

Should you find new ways of handling internal work flow? Change routines? Try to examine systems in the business periodically? Or should you let a smoothly functioning operation continue as is? Seize new technologies or perfect current ones? Systematically budget for R&D or opt for a project basis?

Your aim in this step is to become conscious of what strategies govern your business, what choices you might be able to make about future strategies, and what strategies may be needed as your markets change. This is a groundwork step, one on which you will build further strategies.

Action Plan For:
"The Four Stages of Strategic Planning"

❑ Determine what the marketplace holds for your company in the future.

❑ Think of a one-sentence answer to the question "What business am I in?"

❑ Look at the internal operations of your business in the following areas: financial, marketing, production/ distribution, and personnel development.

❑ Think about what you want out of your business, and list your goals.

❑ List the strategies that currently govern your business in the same areas as the third step above.

Chapter Two:

Choosing Strategies for Your Business

....

In the previous chapter, we focused on the four stages of strategic planning: financial planning (budgets), forecast-based planning, qualitative planning, and finally, a meld of management thinking and strategic thinking that becomes part and parcel of running the business.

The strategic planning process begins with an analysis of the current situation. As you examine the business arena, your assumptions about the future become more precise. As you examine internal operations, ideas for improvement will occur to you. As you list your personal business goals, the lines between what you want for yourself and for your business blend.

Now you must examine strategies.

A strategic plan sets down a range of strategic options, all of which serve to promote the interests of your business under certain sets of external conditions. A strategy which is appropriate for all conditions is appropriate for none; different economic climates call for different strategies. Hence the need for a variety of appropriate strategies.

Since most companies operate without explicit strategies, making your strategies explicit gives you a competitive edge and helps you gain the right market position for your business. "Right" in this context means the position which makes your goals attainable—and your business profitable.

Once you have gone through the process and have considered a variety of possible strategies, these important results will have been gained.

You will: have an understanding of some strategies that might not have appeared as options for your business; begin to think strategically; gain a draft of a strategic plan which expresses your assumptions about the future, helps you position your business to take advantage of the changes you see coming, and makes you more alert to opportunities in the changing marketplace.

This takes effort. You can get help—your banker, your professional advisors and specialized consultants are available to assist you. But the major effort has to come from you.

Summarize business and personal objectives

After you review the results of the previous chapter, summarize the business and personal objectives which you wish to achieve over the next five or ten years.

A strategic plan provides stability in a rapidly changing world. You think through the goals you want to reach. You think about where you are now—and how to get from here to there.

The easiest goals to specify are quantitative. Most of us talk in terms of dollar volume ("I'd like to run a nice little half-million dollar company... A solid twenty million dollar company... Assets of close to a million bucks... Sales increase of $9,000 a month...").

The rule for a tactical business plan is to make goals as specific as possible to show the detailed steps involved in taking a business from $2 million to $4 million over two years, for example.

The function of a strategic plan is to provide the wide framework within which the tactical (business) plan is written. The particular strategies you choose will result in your business following certain tactics designed to implement those strategies.

For this step, list the main objectives you and your company have for the next ten years:

- What sales level do you want to have in ten years?
- What kind of net worth—personal and corporate?
- How many employees?
- What kind of facilities?

On a non-quantitative level, other questions of equal or greater importance have to be raised. Some of these were covered in the previous chapter. Of particular importance are questions of market positioning, type of business, and product mix pricing.

Some of the questions are quite abstract. What kind of workplace do you foresee? Debates about Quality of Working Life, Theory X or Y, Japanese or Theory Z management, for example, are involved here. What management styles are going to work? What will happen in the all-important marketplace? What about corporate responsibility in non-business areas?

> *Figure 2.1*
>
> **The Difference between Tactics and Strategies**
>
> | Tactics | Strategies |
> | --- | --- |
> | Concrete | Conceptual |
> | Specific | General |
> | Individual | Complex |
> | Linear | Organic |
> | Sequential | Interactive, systematic |

And some questions are hard to answer: What might the general economy be like in five years? What kinds of technologies and methodologies will be at your disposal? What will the patterns be: inflation, deflation, a mix?

Some questions are too vague to answer, but should be raised: What about decentralist tendencies some people are observing at work? What new life-styles and new attitudes will be present in the work force? Nobody can predict these with certainty—but if you are aware of current thinking on these subjects, you might find your business of the next 20 years.

List a range of strategies

If you do nothing else with this chapter or the last, read and think about the range of options presented on the following pages. They form the heart of your strategic plan. The list has proven itself in hundreds of applications, for businesses of all sizes—as small as $100,000 gross sales, as large as Fortune 500 companies.

Note the format. You can use the list to look at what happened in the past, what you do now, and what you think you might do in the future. Put check-marks next to the strategies—then go back later and expand your thinking about why and how these strategies will be useful.

This form will help you define past and present strategies. It should also be considered as a source of ideas for future strategies.

How many strategies should you consider? That depends—on what your business is, what you see as its resources, possible market traps and opportunities, and on other assumptions about the future. Note that the great majority of the strategies are market-centered. If you can find the right products for the right markets early enough, other problems can be solved. But even the best minds can't sell poor products to the wrong markets.

Figure 2.2

Checklist for Strategic Planning:
Sample Marketing Strategies

Past	Current	Future	Strategy	Probable Consequences, Risks
			Rationalize distribution. Cut back to most efficient network; look at volume, geography, type.	Increased profit margins, lower inventories, some costs go down. May need new investment. Moderate risk.
			Develop the market. Create demand for a brand new product.	Very high marketing costs, may increase receivables, impacts P&L, hinders cash flow. Large expense budget. High risk—but high reward if successful.
			Penetrate the market. Increase market share; lower price, product line mix made broader, more service and sales personnel, increase advertising.	Increased marketing and sales expense, need more working capital, more capital investment if growth in capacity needed, reduction in short-term earnings. High risk.
			Promote new products to present market. Develop, broaden, or replace products in product line, sell to present market.	Lower unit cost, increased inventory, sales volume, profit and cash flow. Some capital investment needed, increased development, design, and manufacturing costs. Moderately high risk.
			Seek new markets, same products. Expand existing markets by geography (abroad) or type for existing markets.	Increased sales volume, profit margins as unit costs drop, new market grows. Higher short-term selling costs, some cash flow help. Modest capital investment, increased working capital. High risk.

Sample Marketing Strategies

Past	Current	Future	Strategy	Probable Consequences, Risks
			Develop new products for new markets. Invest in developing, manufacturing, and marketing products unrelated to product line for new markets.	Increased sales volume, costs, profits (if successful), has same problem as a new business if products unrelated to current line. Need more working capital, may need new capital investment, increase in sales and marketing costs. Willingness to accept lower sales totals. High risk.
			Rationalize market. Prune back to most profitable segments, higher volume segments; concentrate marketing focus.	Reduced sales volume, increased profit margins, lower working capital needs, increase cash flow as % of sales, decrease receivables. Willingness to accept lower sales totals. Moderate risk.
			Maintain products and market share. Business continues as before: same products, same market.	Increase at industry growth rate, stable short-term profit margins, decrease working capital over time, increased cash throw-off over time, may lower unit costs. Low risk.

Checklist for Strategic Planning:
Sample Management Strategies

Past	Current	Future	Strategy	Probable Consequences, Risks
			Cut costs. Reduce costs uniformly through management edicts.	Increased profit margins, achieve lowest possible return of all possible strategies. Needs excellent implementation to apply intelligently. Moderate risks due to arbitrary nature of cutbacks—may have invidious consequences.
			Abandon unit. Sell or liquidate unit because it doesn't fit with company—or because it is worth more to someone else.	Improve cash flow from sale of assets, create possible morale problems in rest of organization. Low risk.

Sample Management Strategies

Past	Current	Future	Strategy	Probable Consequences, Risks
			Rationalize product line. Narrow profit line to most profitable terms.	Reduce sales volume, improve working capital, profitability, may lead to underutilizing assets in short term. Hard to give up old winners. Low to moderate risk.
			Pure survival. Hunker down to meet adverse conditions by eliminating or paring down some aspects of	Reduce sales volume, considerably reduce costs, improve ROI short term, improve cash flow temporarily. Courage needed, moderate risk due to possible loss of market share, some danger from creditors and other trade sources.

Sample Financial Strategies

Past	Current	Future	Strategy	Probable Consequences, Risks
			Pause in action. Slow down or establish a one-year moratorium on new capital investment; normal maintenance of business.	No effect on sales short term, may disrupt growth plans, weaken business over long term, decreased sales and earnings if pause too lengthy. Courage and large measure of steadfastness. Low risk.

Sample Production Strategies

Past	Current	Future	Strategy	Probable Consequences, Risks
			Improve technology. Improve operating efficiency through technological improvements in physical plant, equipment or process.	Decreased variable costs and increased fixed costs—an overall reduction can considerably increase profits, affect sales volume slightly. Low to high capital investment. Low to moderate risk depending on the extent to which the particular technology is proven.

Sample Operating Strategies

Past	Current	Future	Strategy	Probable Consequences, Risks
			Improve methods and functions. Invest in new methods by adding new "soft" technology: e.g., new patterns of work flow, CAD/CAM, production planning & inventory control, etc. so as to improve effectiveness and/or efficiency.	Improve operating performance, improve functional rather than product costs. Expense investment. Creative thinking needed. Low to moderate risk.

Test strategies for consistency, feasibility and coherence

Now you have a list, perhaps tentative, of strategies which may fit your company and personal goals, and an explicit set of assumptions about future markets, products, and economic circumstances. Prudence demands you be realistic. Use good, bad, and most probable scenarios as a way to hedge your bets.

For any set of strategies, envisage how they will affect your business. What resources are needed? What will happen to sales, profitability, personnel and other assets if the plans are achieved? What are the risks in terms of present and future hazards? What are the rewards?

Three criteria for making choices between competing strategies are:

- Consistency
- Feasibility
- Coherence with goals

Consistency demands that your strategies fit with each other. You can't simultaneously increase capital spending and improve cash flow while prohibiting new investment, new borrowing, and sale of assets. It can't be done—but it has been tried. Look at the consequences and requirements of your potential strategies systematically. Consider them as they would interact with each other. Seek consistency.

Feasibility demands that the strategies make business sense. Some projects may call for skills that are not available, capital that is not going to appear on time, penetration of markets already well served. A clever management follows the rules of guerrilla warfare. Choose where and when to fight. Never engage the enemy unless you're in a highly dominant position. Make sure you don't overextend your supply lines. Avoid wars of attrition. Don't get cornered. This doesn't mean that you shouldn't have dreams—but it does mean that you should be aware of the risks involved, that you should know how to muster the necessary resources, and that you find market niches which can be easily defended.

Coherence with goals demands that the strategies actually further the achievement of the goals. Too much emphasis is placed on quarterly profit and loss performance at the expense of long-term goals such as meeting the real needs of the market. If your set of strategies does nothing more than keep your efforts centered on meeting real market needs at a profitable price, it will be immensely valuable to you.

Make the goals as clear as you can. Some will be highly conceptual; most should be qualitative; some will be expressed in dollars and dates.

Then test each strategy with this simple question: Will this strategy, if implemented, help make these goals achievable?

Choose the simplest strategies for your business

Apply Occam's Razor, an old philosophical tool, to your choice of strategies: Given two competing strategies, choose the simplest. You can get as complicated as you might desire with fine details—but that will be tactical activity. Strategically, aim for simplicity.

Why? Complex strategies don't work—they are hard to communicate and present too many chances to go wrong.

Simple strategies tend to be effective. If your employees and markets know what you are doing, and can understand and see that you do what you promise, you have the beginning of an effective strategy.

Most of your competitors won't be able to resist trying to improve on what you do by making it a bit fancier, a bit more complicated, a little bit more sophisticated.

Implement strategies; revise as needed

Involve your colleagues and employees in the strategic planning process. They'll help implement it. Ram it down their throats and they'll resist it—and you'll have forgone their cooperation.

Figure 2.3

A Case Study

Type of business: Armored car and courier service

Dollar volume: 1.5 million

In this case, management decided they needed an objective, rational look at a variety of problems that had developed. Their banker was reluctant to lend additional funds until further planning had been done.

Analysis of the current situation:
There was no question that the company was run by a brilliant entrepreneur, but there was a lack of focus, a lack of direction. They felt the need to separate symptoms from problems.

They knew that undercapitalization was having a severe impact on the company and that their receivables were inadequately managed.

What their strategic planning efforts revealed:

- Their competitors, even the larger, better-financed ones, always billed weekly in advance. This gave the management the leeway, without raising the customers' eyebrows, to do the same.

- To expand, the company needed a management system in which productive people could advance. They needed a "career ladder" and an incentive program.

- A computer was becoming a necessity.

The results?

- Cash flow greatly improved as a result of changed billing procedures. No customers were lost.

- A management system is now in place; two new managers were hired.

- A plan for a computer was drawn up and the appropriate system purchased.

- The company now has $3 million in sales and profits are up.

The most effective implementation method is to set a timetable. Once you have come to a set of strategies that meets the selection criteria, have thought it through enough to feel comfortable, and have communicated the decisions to your staff, put the strategies to work. Your ultimate aim is to get everyone to think in terms of the long-term survival and profitability of the company. You don't have to race ahead—but a definite starting date helps get the strategy operational.

Implementing strategies is a tactical activity. See Figure 2.1 for a review of the differences; they apply here.

You will have to revise your plans. Do so—but slowly, and only if you see compelling reasons. A plan that shifts with every pressure is useless.

Strategic planning relies heavily on your ability to look ahead. It demands that you draw on current and reliable information sources. Read, talk to people, pay attention to trends, reflect on the things you learn. Consider the implications of social change, shifts in populations, trends in various industries, and the economy.

Your strategic plan provides a set of strategies which, if followed, should help you achieve more than you may realize is possible.

Action Plan For:
"Choosing Strategies for Your Business"

❏ Review the range of options for what you might do in the future, and elaborate upon why and how these strategies will be useful.

❏ Consider how your strategies will interact with one another; seek consistency.

❏ Determine whether your strategies are feasible, and whether the appropriate resources and skills are available to you at the appropriate time.

❏ Determine whether the strategies you'll implement further the achievement of your goals.

❏ Choose simple strategies to be effective.

❏ Involve your colleagues and employees in the strategic planning process by setting a timetable.

❏ Revise your strategies when you need to.

Chapter Three:

The Marketing Plan

··

In the last two chapters, you took a fresh look at your business, your assumptions about the future, and your personal goals. You also began thinking about the route you'll follow to achieve these goals.

The most important map you can draft is a marketing plan. One that's geared to your business and its existing product and service lines, markets and finances can keep your business on course, even in a fluctuating economy.

First and foremost, be aware of your options and limitations. Looking for a market gap and developing a way to fill it is fine for a start-up (or for a business which has managed to create a positive cash flow plus a pool of skills which can be drawn on). But for most of us, the best marketing opportunities come directly from our ongoing business.

Second, analyze your products and services. Try to look at them the way prospective customers do. If possible, enlist your customers as marketing helpers. Your salespeople can help. Your suppliers, bankers, and other professional advisors can help. The aim is to discover new applications for your goods and services, new ways to put the existing strengths of your business to work.

Third, scrutinize your current markets. The rule is that 80 percent of your profits come from 20 percent of your accounts. This general rule is riddled with exceptions—but some of your customers are far more profitable for you than others. You may discover that some of the least profitable business comes disguised as major orders, while some apparently small orders emerge as major contributors.

Identify where the money really comes from, and you take a major step towards targeting the market.

Fourth, systematically segment and categorize your markets, both current and prospective. As you combine and recombine various groups, you will perceive relationships between them that will help you spot new marketing strategies.

Fifth, examine the competition, current and potential. Look beyond the obvious; if your business is vulnerable, the most severe damage comes when and where you least expect it. Glean good ideas from the competition, apply them in your business, identify the mistakes the others are making, and avoid them in your operation. That will give you the best of all possible competitive situations. A clean, well-run, aggressive business—especially if it is forward-looking—won't be caught off guard.

Sixth, try to match skills and applications of your business's strengths with the market segments available to your firm at this time. Personnel, distribution, and available funds are limits to consider. (Your competition is probably doing the same, though not systematically.) The aim: to find the best mixture of product/service lines, markets, and competitive positioning for your business at this time (while keeping options open for the future).

Seventh, convert all insights, information and plans to a written marketing plan that provides measurable goals, citing precise dollar and/or unit sales goals to reach within a definite time. As with any planning effort, a written plan is an advance over the far more frequent "I've thought about it..." plan that the majority of small and mid-sized businesses run on.

Eighth, implement and monitor the plan, changing it to suit the exigencies of the future. No plan is going to be 100 percent accurate and successful—but by taking the time to formulate a marketing plan, you will gain an immediate edge on your opponents. Writing the plan down will sharpen it up, make it more precise and less prone to error. Good use of the plan will solidify and increase your ability to outdo the competition.

Use your (and your employees') experience first, and then turn to more specialized resources such as market research firms or specialized marketing consultants. Use what you have at hand to identify areas where professional marketing skills will be useful. There is no sense in paying for work that you could have done more swiftly, less expensively, and better. As an example, a publishing company once used a marketing firm to do a study of certain markets which turned out to duplicate information they already had. The cost: six weeks and $6,000.

Identify options and limitations

Your marketing plan should reflect the limitations your business faces but identify options open to you. Avoid getting too bogged down in the "Can't do it" syndrome. Start by identifying your options.

Beware of dismissing options that at first glance seem to be unrealistic. They may turn out to be the future of your company.

How do you seek options? First, look to your personnel—their skills and energies are the basis of company growth in the short term. While you may always hire outside talent, the time and opportunity costs involved will be high. After a few years of operation, a company has a built-in momentum that is extraordinarily hard to change. People develop fixed ways of doing things, of looking at problems and markets, of thinking about product lines and future additions to products and services that fit in very closely with the way the company does business.

The unused or underutilized skills of your employees spell the difference between being moderately profitable and being an exciting, highly profitable business.

Second, ask your customers. Read trade journals. Get all the information you can—and jot the products/goods/services ideas down.

Remember, the more ideas you sift through, the better your chances of identifying the right products for your business and your markets.

Objectivity about the limitations of your business is only slightly less important than opening your mind to new ideas. The main limitations are (in this order): managerial personnel, skilled personnel, and money.

The most dangerous threat to small growing businesses is that they outgrow the management before management knows what's happening.

The second hurdle is skilled personnel. Skilled production people need time to develop new patterns to accommodate new production needs. You can't sell a service if you don't have the trained personnel. But it also crops up in retail operations; familiarity with product lines is an important sales tool.

Take into account that new marketing ideas are disruptive because of time involved in training and adjustment.

All of the above cost money—sometimes a lot more than anticipated. While this is a severe problem for a company with a skimpy cash flow and not enough capital, for most ongoing businesses the cost of developing new items for the market is part of the cost of doing business. (Bankers know this. A substantial part of the demand for commercial loans comes from the working capital needs created by new products/goods/services development.)

Analyze products and services

A careful product and/or service line analysis is the next part of a marketing plan.

Start by becoming as familiar as possible with your current products. In most businesses, the market gains will come from new applications of old products.

That's why you need to be thoroughly familiar with the products and services you now offer. By asking yourself what these products have to offer—and asking your customers, sales force, suppliers, and anyone else who might have an interest in your business—you may find the germ of the new applications that are tomorrow's sales.

Why do people buy your products rather than someone else's competing models? What else can you offer them that is congruent with your present production, sales, and support staff, as well as your product lines?

Figure 3.1

Product/Service Line Analysis

1. List the products and/or services you market.

2. What is the purpose of each?

3. For each one: Is it a breadwinner? Now or in the future? Is it past its prime? Should it be discontinued? Should it be given more support?

4. What are its particular advantages and disadvantages as compared with competitive goods and services?

5. What makes it unique?

6. What improvements have been made to the product or service lately?

7. What new products are being contemplated? As new products? As products to fill out a line? As a way to meet competition?

8. What are possible substitutes for your goods? What new developments (technological or other) might result in new products, new competitive possibilities for next year? Next five years?

9. Can you list at least five new applications for your products?

Be objective. Look at your products from a customer's viewpoint. (If you serve an institutional or corporate market, keep in mind that a purchasing agent does the buying—not some amorphous institutional mass. People buy things.) You may appreciate the care, technical expertise, and devotion that went into producing your widget. Your customers are probably more interested in how they can use that item and at what cost. They will be comparing it with other products. No product is so unique that it lacks competition.

Remember, new ideas are often more valuable than yesterday's products.

As an example of an unusual application of a product, basketballs are used as ball valves in some nuclear installations. Basketballs have to meet high standards for toughness, resilience, uniformity, and abrasion resistance.

Scrutinize current markets

Who are your present customers? If you can't answer this, drop everything until you can; it is the basis of all your marketing efforts.

Ask—and ask again: Who is buying which products from you? Why are they buying them? Which customers are profitable? Which are not?

That third question is not easy to answer. You must know which products and which markets are making money for you.

A modest investment of your time can make this information readily available. Paying for this information is a necessary business expense, not a luxury.

How do you gain the information about your current market? Ask your sales personnel. Examine your receivables, shipping records, billings, and time records. Look for contributions to overhead and profit, not just sales levels.

You can ask your customers directly (as an example, have sales clerks offer a card to fill out or suggest signing for special mailings). You can ask your customers indirectly; marketing students from local colleges do a good job in assembling this kind of program, and it helps everyone involved. Aim to develop customer profiles so you can segment and categorize your present markets and get a lead on future ones.

Ask your customers why they buy from you, who might use the same or similar products and how you can better meet their needs. By centering

Figure 3.2

A Case Study

As part of the evaluation of a new product or service idea, look at what it could do to the available management time. One company, for example, found that a new product line created two distinct strains on management. First, the level of administrative detail rose dramatically, calling time away from ongoing projects at a crucial point; second, the sales force was strained almost to the breaking point, which resulted in both sales lags (as managerial time was siphoned off to training and introduction work) and a lot of minor production headaches. This combination of problems happens with almost any new project. If you are aware that more overhead (administrative) time will be involved, both in production and sales, many problems can be averted.

this kind of request on two sets of customers (profitable ones, who buy a lot with little cost to you, and marginal customers, who could be upgraded to profitable ones), you are apt to find out what you are doing right, what you could be doing better, and how your products are perceived as desirable.

Failure to ascertain who the profitable customers are leads many companies to squander market opportunities and pursue chimerical profits.

Your aim: finding more and more profitable customers.

Figure 3.3

Some Market Segmentation Criteria

Individual

☐ age ☐ gender ☐ race ☐ hobbies ☐ lifestyle ☐ education ☐ social class ☐ occupation ☐ income levels ☐ family life cycle

Business

☐ location ☐ structure ☐ sales level ☐ special requirements ☐ distribution patterns ☐ number of employees ☐ manufacturer/service/retail/wholesale ☐ SIC (Standard Industrial Classification)

Systematically segment and categorize markets

Segmenting and categorizing your market makes sense for even the smallest business. If you know which customers are buying what products, and what the impact of these identified customers is on your profits, you can get to know a lot about them. Then look for more customers with the same characteristics—customers who will buy your goods and services.

Some businesses are set apart by the care and thoroughness with which the raw insights ("I see more institutional sales this month, don't I?") are converted to useful information ("Sales to schools are up 15 percent—or $8,000—over last month, through a direct mailing to principals of schools in metro areas in the Southeast...").

The list in Figure 3.3 may suggest some criteria by which to segment your markets. You have to tailor the approach to fit your business's options and limitations, products, and special market situations. (Many marketing studies are abandoned as too hard before they even start.)

Ask—continually—"Why do these people buy from our company? Why?" Once you understand what motivates people to purchase your products, you will gain: a better idea of other prospects (people with the same profile of wants and needs), new ideas of how your products are perceived in the marketplace, and even ideas for new applications and new products.

Examine the competition

A fine tip-off to the future can be gained from closely and diligently following the competition's efforts. This doesn't mean playing catch-up, however. It means keeping an eye on what they are doing and how they are selling what products—and to whom—at what prices.

You want to learn from their mistakes as well as from their successes. A substantial addition to the effectiveness of your business plan will come from identifying who your competitors are, who is buying from them rather than from you, why that's the case—and then figuring what you can do to recapture those sales. These are very promising prospects, and if you can find out why you aren't getting

---

them and someone else is, you have a chance to pull them into your camp. As a first step, carefully measure market shares—yours, theirs—and then look for trends.

Keep an eye out for those businesses which are not competitors now but could be—particularly if you have a highly profitable market that could be engulfed by a larger, more heavily capitalized business.

If you can find non-competitive businesses (separated, say, by geography) in the same industry as your business, you may be able to get an even clearer reading. In the camera industry, for example, one manufacturer has an annual meeting of representative dealers from distinct locations. The dealers trade bright ideas and mistakes, help one another do better, and (not incidentally) help the manufacturer better understand the needs of the markets he serves.

That's what studying the competition does; it gives you that little bit extra that makes the difference.

Match your business's strengths with the market's

The final step before actually putting ink to paper is to match up, as best you can, the strengths of your business (personnel, resources, products/goods/ services, intangibles such as good distribution relations) to the needs and desires of the markets you choose to serve.

The heart of the marketing plan will be determining which markets afford you the best mix of price and product for your business goals. Following this, outline what steps you must take to increase your market share (new product development and other means).

All of this is done first to allow you to carefully, thoroughly, and wisely match up what your business can afford to do with what the market wants. Nobody— not Procter & Gamble, not General Foods, not IBM—can do more.

Where do you start? List the ten options that make the most sense to you (and to your associates, if you wish more effective cooperation). Rank them—in terms of potential profitability, ease of implementation, fit with present product and service lines, even pricing fit. (Pricing is a major part of your marketing and is covered in Chapters 13 and 14. For now, remember: Profit is a function of both price and costs. It may be more profitable to sell more units at a lower rate, fewer units at a higher rate, or even to offer several different products to get different segments of the market.)

Now match up the market segments and rank them in terms of size, share that you can expect to get for specific products (now, in one year, in two years), and ease of entry and protection.

Figure 3.4

Looking Ahead

It is important to set realistic, short-term goals for your business. These more immediate goals can help you clarify and analyze your longer-range goals. The following checklist provides some questions which may help you pin down plans for the future of your business.

1. What are your marketing goals for the next year in the following areas? The next five years? □ dollar sales □ unit sales □ profits □ market share □ activities to begin □ activities to stop □ customers to drop □ markets to enter □ markets to abandon □ customer base expansion □ production/product improvement □ reputation

2. Rank your principal marketing problems in order of urgency.

3. What major threats and what major opportunities does your company face in the next five years in the following areas? □ products and services □ competitive activity □ customer attitudes □ general business environment.

4. What new competition do you expect within the next five years?

5. What competitors do you expect will decline or disappear within the next year? Five years? Why?

6. What proportion of your sales five years hence will come from new products? New markets?

Since you are looking for the best match of strengths and markets, you will probably find that a process of eliminating the least attractive market mixes will ease the final choice.

Whether you end up with only one new mix or a dozen is unimportant— what is vital is to recognize that your available resources can be stretched only so far, and that you want to use those resources as effectively as you can.

Assemble a written marketing plan

A marketing plan is an adjunct to the broader business planning efforts; it doesn't operate in a vacuum.

A suggested outline:

• Brief description of current markets, products, and/or services.

• Your share of these markets.

• Suggestions for improving market share.

• Suggestions for new products.

• Cost of these suggestions: personnel, training, time, and money.

• Timetable for achieving sales and marketing goals.

Keep it short. Whenever possible, tie down the ideas and suggestions with specific figures, particularly time and costs. One of the most useful marketing plans we've ever seen was six pages long. It described several services to be offered to a specific industry, tied to a monthly schedule of mailings, phone calls, sales, and anticipated cash flows.

You may want to enlist some help in putting together your first marketing plan—after the first one, updating it is simple.

You want your plan to answer the following questions: Who is your market? Why is this a good market for your business? Is that market growing? Shrinking? Stable? What's your share of that market? What is the trend of your share? How can you increase the profitability of your market share?

If you are involved in a manufacturing operation, add answers to: What are your production equipment needs? What are your sources of supply? What are your skilled labor needs? Sales force and office needs?

The really tough trick is to translate the strengths and market insights into a step-by-step approach to entering and profiting from a new market. New prospects, new customers, upgraded orders from old customers, and so on, can be forecast with some accuracy if you do the necessary spadework.

The payoff: controlled growth that won't wreck your business or outstrip its personnel, production, or capital assets.

Implement, monitor and revise the plan

As with any plan, you must put it to work. Sitting on a shelf, a plan will be useless. Marketing campaigns—including communication with the market, advertising, sales strategies and support, distribution, service and repair—demand precise goals. Measure progress by comparing actual accomplishments to these goals.

Finally, plan to revise your marketing plan at least once a year. Goals—and circumstances—change. Your plan must change too—but only after thoughtful analysis.

Action Plan For:
"Developing a Marketing Plan"

❑ Be aware of your options, limitations and opportunities.

❑ Analyze your products and services to find new applications for the future.

❑ Look at your current customers and determine who is buying what, why, and which customers are profitable.

❑ Segment your customers to determine why they buy from your company.

❑ Follow the competition's efforts.

❑ Figure out which markets afford you the best mix of price and product in light of your goals, and eliminate the least attractive market mixes.

❑ Write down your marketing plan.

❑ Periodically measure your progress, and revise your plan when necessary.

Chapter Four:

Analyzing Your Competition

....

Aspects of your marketing plan that demand ongoing attention are the subjects of the next two chapters. The first—learning about your competition—is invaluable for any business owner who wants to expand his or her company. Your competition can teach you a lot, thereby strengthening your position in the marketplace.

There are three distinct times when you should be concerned about the competition. The first is obvious—when you start up a new business.

When Bill considers opening up Hamburger Villa across the street from Bob's Burger City, he certainly assesses his competitive potential. In fact, if Bill wants to borrow money for the enterprise, chances are that his banker wants some idea who the competition is and how Bill expects to compete against it successfully. Even if Bill is using his own money, you can be sure he thinks this through carefully. Whether he writes it down or not, he performs an analysis of the competition.

The second occasion can be a tense one—when a new competitor arrives on the scene. When you study the competition under these circumstances, you may not have the flexibility and freedom you had before the competitor arrived to maintain or expand your market.

If McDonald's decides to move in a block and a half away from Bob's Burger City, this means trouble for both Bill and Bob. Bill will now have to do a clear, concise analysis of the competition to see how he can maintain his business.

The third occasion is all the time. It means keeping your scouts out and your eyes open, so you'll always allow yourself the time and freedom to prevent competitors from digging into your business. This ongoing monitoring is preventive maintenance, and is your best strategy for protecting your customers and market. Not only is an ounce of prevention worth a pound of cure in forestalling competition and ensuring your survival, but it will also allow you to recognize opportunities when they occur and possibly to expand your market.

When Bob, the owner of Bob's Burger City, decides to retire two years later, Bill can take steps to capture Bob's market, if he knows about it ahead of time. Monitoring the competitive situation can give him the advantage here.

Don't wait for trouble to start. Avoid it.

It is time for you to concentrate on making an analysis of the competition a routine activity. If you do it regularly and correctly, you can often avoid being successfully challenged by new competition. If your business is strong and aggressively run, a potential competitor may back off and choose another location. If the competitor does come in, and you've done your homework correctly, you won't be caught off balance.

The 80-20 rule is a good rule of thumb. Eighty percent of your profits come from 20 percent of your customers. If you can identify that 20 percent and gear your strategy to keeping that group happy, you will be ahead.

List your competition

Who is selling similar products in your marketing area? Who could sell similar products in your marketing area? Who is selling similar products to different markets?

This is your competition!

It is in your best interest to be well-informed about actual and potential competition. Future competitors will be assessing your understanding of your business. If they feel that you do not understand your own market, they'll be more likely to decide to compete with you.

Many businesses are competing for a block of time or a portion of disposable income. Sometimes your most direct competitor is in an unrelated business. The successful business manager recognizes the true competition. What do the movies, bowling, needlepoint, and gardening have in common? They all compete for leisure time. Are you in that contest? Look beyond your most obvious competitors who may not be the competition at all. Your competition is any outfit that can, by its actions, take away a portion of your market.

Analyze the competition

If you get 80 percent of your profits from 20 percent of your customers, so do your rivals. How do they make their money? What do they do differently? In what ways are they similar? Since you just tackled the problem of who your competitors are, you should make an educated guess as to where the competition will be in the future.

If they just bought a large warehouse or a fleet of trucks, they are probably planning to expand. That will affect your business. Local newspapers and magazines can give you more information. Do your competitors frequently run help wanted ads? Are they growing or can't they keep their employees? Look at town or city records. Is the competition seeking any zoning changes? Do increased property taxes signal capital improvements? Sometimes your suppliers or customers know about significant changes.

It is important to understand who the opposing players are. Are the principals young or old? Rich or poor? Local or out of town? Is the owner involved in the business or an absentee owner?

Look at the physical size of the building. Is it much larger than yours? Does it have a larger parking lot or several extra bays for trucks? Try to get an idea as to how much business any new competition expects to do. Don't be afraid to poke around the building (discreetly) if you think that will help. The more you know about your competitors, new ones or ongoing concerns, the better you will be able to respond.

Think of the extensive scouting reports available to major league managers. You need to know how (and how well) the other team plays in order to compete successfully.

Figure 4.1

When to Analyze the Competition

	Frequency	Nature of Analysis
Start-up or purchase	Once	To determine market; satisfy bankers
New competitor threatening	Each time competitor moves in	Crash program to determine survival strategy
Monitoring competitors	Continually	Preventive maintenance to forestall competitors, to seize opportunity

---

Compare yourself to your competitors

Just as you have defined your strengths, your competitors have defined theirs. Chances are that if you have a strong competitor, he or she has also analyzed your weaknesses. Look for the warning signals. If you both sell the same product and your rival's prices are cheaper, it could mean several things. Maybe your competition believes your customers shop on the basis of price. Or maybe your competition pays less for the product in the first place. If your competition advertises service, look at your service. Every firm tries to make itself distinctive in the hopes of carving out a loyal portion of the total market.

Figure 4.2

For Quick Comparison

Customer Seeks	Competition Offers	You Offer
Quality		
Exclusivity		
Lower Prices		
Product Line		
Product Service		
Reliability		
Delivery		
Location		
Information		
Availability		
Credit Cards		
Credit Line		
Warranty		
Customer Advice		
Accessories		
Knowledgeability		
Polite Help		

The most important question you can ask yourself about your business concerns your particular strengths. Something must separate you from your competition if you expect your customers to return. Strengths can be found in many areas. One such strength is quality. Another, exclusivity. Rolls Royce is a good example of both. Volkswagen built an empire based on price and quality. You could rely on availability, as Timex did. These are the most obvious choices.

What does your company do better than the rest of the competition? Service? Reliability? Delivery? Information? What part of the market have you carved out for yourself, and how can you serve it better?

Now that you've determined how good you are, what are your weaknesses? Every company has a set of weaknesses. The best companies deal with them continuously. Are your customers happy with the quality of your product? Are you losing sales because of low inventory levels? Are your employees making sales or killing them? Are your prices too high?

Figure 4.3

Analyzing Advertising

A major tool of competition is advertising. One of the best ways to assess your competition is to pick up a piece of their advertising. What do they stress in their ads? Do they feature price, delivery, reliability? Do they focus on a particular issue because they do it better than you? Is that focus important to the customer?

Another important consideration is where your competition advertises. Do they use newspapers, radio, or trade journals? What impression does their advertising leave on the customer? Is their advertising effective?

Is it time to review your advertising?

This does not mean that you have to fight your competition on every front. Perhaps your distinct advantage is the best one to have. Your central concern is your customers' satisfaction. You know your strengths; emphasize one or more of them. Learn your weaknesses; do what you can to compensate for them.

It is difficult to compare one operation with another, but it is essential. Does your competitor see a weakness in your business or a potential that you have missed in the total market?

How is the competition financed? Did they mortgage a house to open up next to you? Is it a division of a much larger corporation with enough money to really squeeze you? If your new competition is borrowing heavily, will a price war initiated by you put the squeeze on them? Maybe you could add an extra service that they can't afford.

Now, tie this back in to these questions: What is important to your customers and to the market in general? How can you adjust to better serve those needs and at the same time throw the competition off balance?

Figure 4.4

Danger Signs

Your competition is:

- Building a new warehouse
- Purchasing additional property
- Developing a new company image
- Cutting or raising prices
- Remodeling the interior of the store
- Buying new or additional delivery trucks
- Remodeling the exterior of the store
- Stepping up newspaper or radio advertising
- Changing store hours
- Adding salespeople or expanding the market territory
- Providing new information or more complete customer advice
- Providing additional services, such as one-day delivery
- Extending credit
- Redesigning its product
- Conducting a market survey
- Changing its product line, adding or subtracting
- Sponsoring a softball team
- Actively participating in community activities

Your business is:

- Losing customers
- Losing sales volume
- Running into cash flow problems
- Having increased personnel difficulties

Within the industry:

- Technological changes could make some of your products obsolete.
- The experience of similar businesses with similar market segments, located in other geographic areas, has been unfavorable.
- Your product is one that consumer groups are concerned about for ecological or medical reasons.

Seek auxiliary information

Your network of suppliers is a good source of information. If you are in a fairly standardized industry, ask your suppliers if you order the same products as your competition, and in the same ratios. Maybe you are missing out on some important products that would fill out your line and generate more profit. (It is also quite possible that your competition carries products that don't sell and that you shouldn't carry, but it is best to understand the differences.) And don't automatically reject an idea just because your competitor had it first.

Other questions you can ask your suppliers include how your product mix and annual sales compare to that of your competitors. If you sell an awful lot of pink widgets and your competition sells mostly blue ones, is there a way for you to sell more blue ones? Remember, if your competition is as aggressive as you should be, they are asking the same questions.

These activities are not dirty tricks, but standard operating procedure. Whether it's baseball scouting or industrial espionage, it goes on routinely. While suppliers probably shouldn't disclose facts about competition, they often do. And if your supplier does tell you about your competition, it is a safe bet that your competitors could find out the same about you.

Set aside time from your busy schedule to shop the competition or have a trusted delegate do so. In any competition, the more you know about an opponent the better. Have yourself shopped by an objective appraiser—it's a great way to discover strong and weak spots.

Read the trade journals and any literature you can find that relates to your product. You can never be too well-informed; some small fact can be a key piece in solving a problem.

Look outside your immediate area. Competitors become colleagues once they're a certain distance away. You meet them at trade association meetings and they exchange information on how to deal with competition, what to be on the lookout for, and a hundred and one other useful ideas.

Prepare a competitive marketing strategy

Now that you've compared yourself with your competition and know where your strengths and weaknesses are, prepare a marketing strategy that will take advantage of areas where you have the edge over your opponent while correcting your weaknesses.

Decide what needs changing and how you plan to change it. Cost it out, get advice or help where needed, and get going. For example, you might want to:

- Provide 24-hour delivery to anywhere in the city.

- Train clerks to be better informed on product line.
- Emphasize courteousness.
- Improve your image via better advertising.
- Sponsor a summer softball team.
- Organize displays more attractively and efficiently.

The expense of implementing many such strategies is nominal, while the pay-off can be surprisingly rewarding.

Implement strategy; review regularly

This last step is the most important of all. Take action. Don't wait. Each day that you expose a weakness, your competition can grow stronger, and you could lose part of your market.

Make sure that your plan is implemented correctly, then monitor its results to note improvement or sluggishness. If the strategy is working, check to see what it is you're doing well. If not, check for problem areas. In either case, steady checking of the effects of your strategy is critical to ensuring the success in your new marketing plan.

Action Plan For:
"Analyzing Your Competition"

❑ Determine who your competition is—list any organization that can take away a portion of your market.

❑ Learn how your competition does business and makes money as well as what their future plans are.

❑ Figure out your strengths and weaknesses vis-à-vis those of your competitors, and focus on how you can serve your markets better than they can.

❑ Look for additional information about your competitors by talking to suppliers, shopping your rivals, reading trade publications, and attending trade association meetings.

❑ Prepare, implement, and review the marketing strategy that gives you an edge over your competition.

Chapter Five:

Inexpensive Market Research

The second aspect of marketing that's an ongoing job is learning more about your prospective customers. Market research does not have to be expensive to be accurate and valuable. Many businesses can get the information they need with little or no professional assistance. Information about your business's markets is as essential as financial forecasting, but is often overlooked due to the common belief that market studies are only for the highly prosperous corporation.

Market research can be defined as any dependable information that makes you more knowledgeable about the people who buy your products or services, and improves your marketing decisions.

It's not always best to perform the research yourself, but by reviewing the following guidelines, you may be able to boost sales without ever touching the checkbook.

Create market research goals

Before you embark on any form of market research, you must determine what you need to know. What are your basic questions? Figure 5.1 is a checklist designed to help you get started. Scrutinize what you already know about every aspect of your market, including your customers, the products or services you sell, where you sell them, and who your competition is. Some of the answers you seek may appear during this preliminary stage.

Figure 5.1

Basic Market Research Questions

About the buyer	About the competition	About the product
How old?	Market share?	Bought because?
Annual income?	Advertising plan?	Price?
Gender?	Price?	Service?
Ethnic group?	Distribution?	Packaging?
Occupation?	Features?	How will it be used?
Homeowner?	Length of time in business?	How many bought in a year?
Media preferred?		What to improve?

These are only a few basic questions to consider.
Your products/services will dictate others.

Once you have determined precisely what you need to know about your market, make a list and arrange the items in order of importance. This will help you decide how far to go with the research in case your time or money runs short.

Finally, you must determine what you are going to do with your information after it has been gathered. If the value of the information you seek is limited in any way, you should note this in your list of goals and invest your time or money accordingly. If, for example, for Office Machines Services, Inc., you'd like to know how many businesses in your state have two or more typewriters in the office, but currently you do not have distribution capacity to service more than your county, be sure to note that. What is that information worth now? If you are planning a major expansion, it may be essential. But, if you know that you're not planning to expand for another five years, it's worth less.

Get a professional estimate

If the information you want is extremely complicated or time-consuming, a professional marketing firm might turn out to be a better alternative. Whether this is the case or not, you should still present your list of goals to a professional in order to get an estimate.

Marketing consultants will usually spend an hour or two learning about your business and your goals. They will then prepare a proposal that includes a firm price range. This information is essential in determining whether it will be less

---

expensive in the long run to have a professional do the job. It will also help you set a budget for your project.

And professionals will sometimes be your best alternative.

Review less expensive alternatives

Market research alternatives can be divided into three categories. Each one yields data that is valuable but may not be relevant to your project. By reviewing the choices in each area, you will find the methods that will work for your goals. These methods should be checked on the worksheet in Figure 5.2 so they can be easily reviewed.

1. Professional help at lower prices

Professionals do not limit their marketing services to costly, full-length studies. They offer other services that might be all your company needs. See if any of these items would work for you:

Subscriptions to general market studies: Professional marketing firms compile research on general market trends for a wide range of business types. These collections are then sold to large corporations, business associations, or banks. They contain useful information about the broader aspects of particular industries.

Partial task research professionals: Some business consultants will take your list of research goals, help you create a plan for research that you can implement yourself, then interpret the results. These are usually private consultants who will provide these services for a set fee.

Hourly basis consultants: If your need for professional assistance is limited to even fewer tasks, some consultants can be retained on an hourly basis. Be prepared, however, for a slightly greater expense at the first meeting since the consultant will need to take the time to get to know your company.

Computerized data base services: For an hourly rate, data base services use the power of computer communications to scan thousands of data banks for existing information about your trade. Some services will collect this data and interpret it for you.

Multi-client surveys: Several different businesses that serve the same market can combine financial resources to fund one survey that meets all of their needs. Professional marketing companies will help you structure this type of survey.

Omnibus surveys: A research firm allows businesses to buy into the survey on a cost per question basis. Each company only pays for the questions it asks and only receives answers to those questions. This is particularly valuable if your marketing goals are narrow enough to be answered in a few questions. If you only want to know, for example, whether color is important to the buyers of power tools, you can ask just that.

Experts on your board of directors: You can enjoy continuous marketing expertise by placing a marketing expert or business consultant on your board of directors or offering a small amount of stock in the company. This provides advice that can be drawn over a much longer period of time.

Enterprise forums: A popular new event that is appearing in more and more cities is the enterprise forum. These forums are commonly offered on college campuses and give new or growing ventures an opportunity to present their business plans to a panel of experts. The experts always include a marketing professional who will work with the rest of the panel to provide constructive criticism about each plan. The marketing expert will usually have some good advice concerning additional market information that is inexpensive yet valuable.

2. Secondary information

Secondary information is data that already exists concerning a market, even though it wasn't necessarily compiled for marketing purposes. This includes everything from census data to magazine articles and, when used correctly, can provide a wealth of useful information.

The reason there is so much valuable secondary data is that for every important economic activity, there is an association that represents it, a government agency that monitors it, and a magazine that covers it.

There are two categories of secondary information included below. One is information that can be found within the existing company and the other is information that must be gathered from other sources. Both are useful and should be considered.

Customer complaint records: There may be no better way to improve your products or services than by listening to customers' complaints. Repeated complaints are obvious indicators.

Sales records and sales reports: As valuable as what's not working is what is selling well, especially if, through sales reports, you can determine precisely what makes a product sell.

Service invoices: Service invoices, like customer complaints, help pinpoint certain problems that a product line is experiencing.

Census data: Census data is very valuable in a number of ways. Census data can determine economic background, dominant age groups, housing needs, and types of employment, and can provide all of the general information about a particular area that a business needs.

Local government agencies: Census material becomes even more useful when it has already been reduced to manageable size by local agencies like county planning and zoning commissions. These groups not only analyze the target area for market trends, but they also predict the future of that same group. Employees of local agencies are often willing to discuss their data with great patience. Furthermore, copies of their publications are available for very reasonable prices.

Business magazines: These publications cover a vast range of ideas and trades. A little time spent in the library can yield worthwhile information in either a general or specific sense.

Trade journals and directories: These are more specialized than commercial business publications and provide tips on where to get more extensive market data as well as everyday news about a specific trade. These can be highly targeted, like *Beer Marketer's Insights*, for example.

Common economic background survey of competitors: In general, business owners are proud of their accomplishments and are usually happy to share them with someone else. A survey of people in the same business that you're in can bring piles of good data. The survey works best when the owners being asked the questions see no threat from the survey. The best results have occurred when the survey is given to businesses in another part of the country where there is no threat of competition but the market is similar enough to make the results useful.

Competitors' advertising techniques: By reviewing advertising of successful competitors over a period of time, you can often determine what strategies have increased their volume of business and what strategies have failed.

Non-profit organization information: Non-profit groups have to perform the same market research that other businesses do. They often have information about their market that they would share with another company for a small fee.

Concept testing: Customers of an existing business will often offer their opinion concerning a new product. However, care must be taken that only likely users of the product are tested. (You wouldn't ask a vegetarian for comments on your Beef Wellington.)

Systematic observation: A business can learn a great deal about customer behavior by observing certain habits either directly or indirectly. For instance, a radio station did a survey of what radio station commuters preferred by noting where the radio dial was set on cars that were in various service stations for repairs.

3. Self-produced primary research

Self-produced primary research essentially consists of various types of surveys. These surveys can range from professionally administered questionnaires to informal chats with knowledgeable business contacts.

Figure 5.2

What Is Your Current Strategy?

Type of Business _____

Goals of Research _____

_____

Professional Estimate _____

Alternative methods you can use:

_____ Market subscriptions	_____ Partial task consultant
_____ Hourly basis consultant	_____ Computerized data base service
_____ Multi-client surveys	_____ Omnibus surveys
_____ Expert on your board	_____ Enterprise forums
_____ Customer complaints	_____ Sales records and reports
_____ Service invoices	_____ Census data
_____ Local government agencies	_____ Business magazines
_____ Trade journals	_____ Survey of competitors
_____ Competitors' advertising	_____ Non-profit organizations
_____ Concept testing	_____ Systematic observation
_____ University-assisted survey	_____ Customer profiles
_____ Focus groups	_____ Informal personal surveys
_____ Trade shows	_____ Manufacturers and suppliers
_____ Mall interviews	

If the primary research you need requires extensive collection of data, then you will need some professional assistance.

University-assisted surveys: Colleges and universities across the country have Small Business Institutes that specialize in studying small businesses. As a result, these programs are constantly seeking new businesses to work with for the benefit of the program and the business.

Small business programs serve more than 8,000 small businesses each year. One of the most valuable services they offer is helping the small business implement market surveys. With the help of the residing professor, business majors and graduate students can complete your research for 10 percent of the cost of the professionals in many cases. Furthermore, they are consistently well-controlled and yield reliable data.

Customer profiles: Another useful primary tool is the creation of the customer profile. By comparing the profile to available secondary data, a business can often reach many conclusions about its market.

Focus groups: Informal discussions conducted with eight to twelve customers or business experts about your products and services can often iron out many of the problems of a new idea before it hits the shelf. These groups are another idea that works especially well on college campuses.

Informal personal surveys with customers: Keeping in mind that any information provided by a customer is subjective, a business can still find answers to certain questions from this source.

Trade shows: There is more data available at a trade show than most people think. Besides seeing your competitors display their strategy, the assortment of people in attendance can offer an endless supply of insight into your trade.

Discussions with manufacturers and suppliers: Who knows your trade better than the people who service or supply it? This source is often overlooked. And, because these individuals might want your business, they are usually willing to spend a fair amount of time answering your questions.

Mall interviews: Finally, if you are attempting to determine your potential clientele, try going where many professionals get their information: the shopping mall. Because of the variety of stores in a mall, a survey is assured an indicative cross-section of respondents, at least for retail goods.

Estimate the cost of performing the research yourself

Using Figure 5.2, you can see how many alternative research methods are germane to your needs. Now it is time to review these alternatives.

Ideally, the items you checked will be a balance of easily accessible information and time-consuming research. If much of the data you desire is readily available and need only be enhanced by a brief survey, you will probably decide to go ahead with your own project. However, if the majority of items you selected require great amounts of time and research, doing it yourself may not be worth the price.

You must weigh the cost of performing the market research yourself to the benefit of the results. The second part is relatively simple. Using your set of market research goals, you can get a fairly strong idea of how your study will improve your marketing decisions. Determining the cost of the research is a bit more difficult.

Costs of devoting time and energy to market research are measured in different ways, depending on your particular situation. For instance, if you have a burgeoning company that is waiting for the study results to determine whether or not to implement a new product, then time is of the essence, and a professional study may be more efficient and timely. Furthermore, if production is hindered while you devote your time to research instead of management, then the cost may again be too great.

However, if your business is still in the start-up phase or if funds are low and slow production leaves you with employees who could be helping with research instead of just putting in their hours, then the cost is minimal compared to the usefulness of the study. This is a decision that is made by you alone, so be sure to consider every hidden cost before deciding.

Select the research plan that will work for you

Having compared the possibilities of completing your own market study to the price of a professional, you'll no doubt learn a great deal about the importance of market research. It may work out that either alternative is too costly if you wish to attain all of your marketing goals. If this is the case, a reasonable alternative is to focus on only a few goals each year. If this is the strategy, and the research is implemented by you and your company, you will become more proficient at obtaining and analyzing data.

Even if your study is limited by time and budget, any research you perform will enhance your market knowledge, and every little bit helps.

Once you have your set of market research goals close at hand and are prepared to devote some time to research, the following steps will guide you through the process of completing your market study.

Gather secondary information

Of the numerous secondary sources you may be able to tap, the most obvious place to start is within your own company. Begin by looking at customer complaints, sales records and reports, and service invoices.

The next step is to gather data from other sources. These include:

- Utility companies
- *American Demographics* (a monthly magazine)
- Planning commissions—regional; county
- Chambers of Commerce, which have extensive demographic information for their areas

The various forms of government information and commercial publications are detailed in a useful collection of reference books. Learning how to perform any of this type of research is made much easier with the help of a librarian.

Collect your primary data

The majority of primary data is gathered through a survey. Surveys ask specific questions in order to yield equally specific information. This type of data is collected in three methods: direct mail, telephone, or door-to-door visits.

Telephone and door-to-door surveys enjoy the advantage of immediate response. There is no time lag between questioning and answers. They are, however, more costly to implement, requiring personal contact with each respondent.

Direct mail surveys are quicker and less expensive to implement. However, there is an indefinite period of time between mailing and response, and virtually no way of predicting the number of recipients who will even take the time to answer your questions.

As a result, the most successful surveys are those that make use of the benefits of both types of surveys. A follow-up phone survey, asking if the target group received the questionnaire and if they have completed it, has yielded the most efficient rate of return.

There are so many important details to be considered when conducting a survey that some form of assistance is almost essential. As we mentioned, partial task or hourly basis consultants can provide you with this expertise. But there is less expensive help available. Universities are always looking for small businesses to work with. Marketing classes will help you create and implement a quality survey. There are also books available that demonstrate how a survey should be organized, including the kinds of questions you should ask for your type of business.

If you plan to conduct a survey, you should consider these types of assistance. You should also become acquainted with the following general guidelines so that you will be even better prepared to meet and talk knowledgeably with your advisors.

Specify objectives: Now more than ever you need to know what information you are seeking.

Train your survey staff: If you are conducting the survey using your own employees, they must know how to perform their research. Your survey advisors can help you train them quickly.

Ask the right questions: Your questions must give you the answers you seek. For instance, a brewery should find out if the survey respondents like beer before they solicit opinions about how their brand tastes.

Stick to the rules: You must correctly apply the principles and methods of data collection. If you don't conduct your survey as scientifically as possible, your data will be much less reliable.

Figure 5.3

A Word on Getting Help

If, on the worksheet, you tended to lean more toward computerized data base services, focus groups, or multi-client and omnibus surveys, then you'll probably need at least partial help from professionals.

Perhaps you have chosen to do your market survey all on your own. Even so, some experienced assistance will help. Librarians, colleges, even high schools are all resources available to you. We suggest that you at least get an estimate for the services of an hourly-basis or partial-task consultant. Consider all of the benefits of a professional before making your decision. For instance, if you retain a business consultant on a part-time basis to help you with your survey, that individual will have a chance to get to know your company and, as a result, be able to more easily assist you with other types of business problems in the future.

Make the survey easy to complete: Multiple-choice questions are preferred when possible. People aren't wild about spending hours of their time completing a survey for a total stranger.

Combine survey techniques: If you are preparing a mail questionnaire, give the respondents some advance notice in the form of a postcard. Enclose a self-addressed, stamped envelope for their reply, and follow up your mailing with a phone call. All of these methods will enhance your rate of return.

Do yourself a favor: Make the survey easy to tabulate. The harder it is to keep score of questions, the longer the process of collecting and interpreting.

With a bit of careful planning, you will achieve a highly effective survey that will yield some valuable results. Meanwhile, don't give up on informal data collection. Be sure to visit trade shows, talk to manufacturers and suppliers, and seek customer opinions. This informal research will serve to support the findings of your questionnaire. One word of warning, however—be sure you like talking to people. If you don't do well with informal chats and social gatherings, send someone who does.

Organize and analyze your research

Now that you've gathered this mountain of paper, it is time to tailor it into a useful research package. The weeding process includes the following steps:

Look for relevant data: Much of the information you gather, especially secondary data, will not be relevant to your research goals. It may be interesting but not necessarily important. Set aside any knowledge that is not germane to your immediate marketing needs.

Examine for objectivity: Much of the information you have gathered may not be objective. Customer complaints and informal personal surveys rely too heavi-

---

ly on biased opinions to be completely predictable. On the other hand, census data and survey responses are less affected by individual bias and therefore more objective. Both sources of information are valuable, but it is best to rely on subjective information only as support for the more general findings of objective research. The two types of information should be separated to further organize your package.

Analyze for consistency: Compare the results of different methods of data collection. Find out if suppliers say the same thing about the market that your survey concludes. Compare competitors' prices to the economic background of the target area. Chances are you'll detect some accurate trends. Furthermore, you can judge the reliability of your various sources by comparing them to each other.

Read between the lines: With a little help from experienced researchers, you can extrapolate the data you have to yield even more information. For instance, by combining census statistics on median income with percentage of homeowners versus renters, a landscape contractor can determine if his services are affordable or even required in particular areas of his target market.

Quantify your results: You can quickly see which data is quantitative and which is not. Quantitative information is simply any data that can be counted. Qualitative information, however, is more subjective and harder to organize. The best way to organize qualitative information is to list it and look for common opinions that might be counted together.

After following these basic steps, you should be able to list some general observations about your research. They should be organized so that you can easily find the source in your research. With list in hand, you can start making decisions.

You may want to consult an expert for help when it comes to interpreting data.

Put your results to work

By using your market research wisely, you can proceed with a plan in confidence. If you followed each step properly, your research will reflect the market accurately. However, cautious decision-making should still be the rule.

Whether your market study was self-produced or purchased from a professional, it is not infallible. Don't place the entire future of your company on the line because of what you are now able to predict. Markets can change in an instant.

The best strategy is a good plan, providing enough options for the future to warrant against unpredictable changes. A market study used in this manner will only yield greater success.

The Case of Able Builders

John Able and his brother owned a small construction company that specialized in custom homes and home improvements. Business was getting worse in their first location due to a depressed local economy, so they decided to move their operation to a more stable region.

Before Able Builders could simply pack up and move, information was needed about the target area that was chosen. Cash in the business was scarce, and Able found that he could not afford a professional market study. Marketing professionals in the area estimated that it would cost about $3000 to achieve all of the marketing goals Able Builders had established. As a result, Able decided to complete his own market study. He had been working on a business plan to be implemented in their new location, and was also enrolled in a small business management course at a local university.

Able began his research with the state census records from his school library and by writing local planning and zoning offices. The local agencies sent him a summary of statistics for his target area along with their General Development Plan. Able compared these statistics to growth projections he found in a marketing magazine. The two were very consistent. All of this information cost a total of $49.60.

Able's next step was to attend a local enterprise forum where other businesses were submitting their plans for criticism. After the forum, Able approached a marketing expert who was on the panel. Following his advice, Able contacted a business consultant who was a friend of the family. The consultant agreed to provide advice on a part-time basis in return for one percent of the company's stock.

By combining the assistance of this consultant with the knowledge of his business professor, Able produced a questionnaire for people in the construction business. He administered the survey by mail to the market adjacent to his target area. The survey enjoyed a 12 percent rate of return and provided Able with a great deal of information about the construction business in that part of the country. Furthermore, it only took Able eight hours to produce, administer, and tabulate the survey. Paper, printing, and postage totaled $68.56.

Well equipped with this information, Able was then ready to travel to the target area to find a place to live and a location for the business. He spent ten days in the area, staying with a friend and borrowing his friend's car part of the time. The entire trip, including plane tickets, cost $285.55 and yielded much more than market information.

Able canvassed the entire target area, speaking to virtually every realtor, developer, and building supply company. He also spoke to several banks about applying for business loans, visited with the local building association, Neighborhood

---

Figure 5.4

Able Builders: Market Research Cost Comparison

Professional estimate based on market research goals:

Part 1:	Socioeconomic back-ground of target area:	$ 250.00
Part 2:	Survey of construction companies and a full report on the area competition:	$ 600.00
Part 3:	Formulation of a strategy for competing; service provided by the hour, $150.00 minimum charge:	$ 150.00
Minimum fee:		$ 1000.00

Housing Authority officials, and Home Improvement Commissions. He even managed to sit down with the author of the General Development Plan to get a personal feeling for the target area.

When Able returned home, he took with him a lease on a house, a stack of market research that verified his previous findings, and several important business connections. Thus, when Able Builders opened its new operation, it was immediately awarded contracts by many of the individuals who had met John Able during his previous trip and were impressed with his company's spirit and organization. This was one major bonus of the market study that no professional service could offer.

Able performed most of his research in the evenings and weekends, taking off only one week to travel to the area. As a result, he felt that the benefits of his market research far outweighed the cost of his labor and an actual cash investment of $403.71.

Able Builders: Market Research Goals

1. To gain a detailed picture of the socioeconomic background of the target area.

Figure 5.5

Able Builders: Actual Cash Cost of Market Study

Secondary Information:

U.S. Census Summary Statistics	$ 8.00
General Development Plan and	
Zoning Manual $ 24.00	
Maps	$ 17.60
	$ 49.60

Materials:

Envelopes (both mailing and	
return)	$ 11.81
Printing costs	$ 12.00
Postage	$ 44.75
	$ 68.56

Travel Expenses:

Airline tickets	$ 123.00
Rental car (two days)	$ 26.55
Other living expenses	$ 136.00
	$ 285.55
Total cost:	$ 403.71

---

2. To examine the different types of residential construction that are currently popular in the area and what the future trend of construction work will be.
3. To gain a complete understanding of the competition in the area, including number of competing companies, work preferences, costs of materials and labor, successful tactics, and reasons for failure.
4. To find out the best way for a small but growing venture to gain a decent share of the market and enhance its exposure when it has limited capital to contribute to such projects.

Able Builders: Planned Usage for Completed Study

1. To complete a thorough business plan that details the next five years of activity. Included in this plan will be a complete strategy for competing with the better-known and established companies.
2. To gain a better conception of the optimum working size of a residential construction company and determine what services yield the most successful operation.
3. To begin immediate implementation of useful business contacts made during the market study.

Action Plan For:
"Inexpensive Market Research"

❑ Determine what you need to know about your market and prioritize your list.

❑ Present this list to a professional and get an estimate.

❑ Review less expensive alternatives like using only specific professional services, looking for useful information from secondary sources, and doing surveys yourself.

❑ Estimate the cost of performing the research yourself, then choose the research plan that will work for you.

❑ Gather data from secondary and primary sources; get professional help when it's needed.

❑ Organize and analyze your research.

❑ Put your results to work.

Chapter Six:

Establishing an Advertising Structure

....

Once you've found new sources of potential customers, your challenge is then communicating with them and motivating them to ultimately buy your product or service. This, in a nutshell, is the mission of advertising.

Where does effective advertising come from?

Although creativity gets all of the credit, a functional analysis of the advertising process reveals that attitudes, structure, and organization are far more important.

Successful advertising results more from good management than creative genius. An effective advertising manager does not have to be able to create good advertising. But an effective Advertising Manager does have to be able to recognize it and extract it from the efforts of others.

Creative people—copywriters, artists, photographers, and the like—do not and cannot operate in a vacuum. They require structure and they require support. Structure is necessary to channel and motivate their creative energies and abilities. This channeling not only focuses their abilities in directions appropriate to the advertiser's long-term and short-term needs, but also motivates them to perform to the limits of their ability.

Believe in advertising, but understand its limitations

Effective advertising begins with proper attitudes. The most important attitude is an appreciation of the limits of advertising. Advertising must never be viewed as a miracle cure which can instantly generate sales and turn around a dying business. If product integrity is lacking, all the advertising in the world won't save the product.

Likewise, advertising is futile if the market doesn't want the product.

Be truthful and straightforward

Responsibility is the second most important attitude which must be present if advertising is to succeed. Responsibility refers to coherence between an advertisement and the product or service it describes. The closer an ad approaches the reality of the product or service being offered, the more effective it is.

Effective advertising is characterized by deceptive simplicity. The product or service is described as simply as possible, in terms a prospective buyer can easily understand and relate to. Technical terms are used only as necessary to support an argument. Every aspect of the ad is prepared from the customer's point of view.

Responsibility also refers to management's willingness to commit the resources necessary to accomplish a given advertising task. Many firms have no difficulty making hard or tangible investments in people, inventory, tools, or buildings. These same firms, however, once having developed competitively strong products, find it difficult to make the intangible investments required to create the proper advertising message and place it often enough in media where the message will reach potential buyers.

Replace opinion with fact

The third attitude—and perhaps the one most difficult to attain—is a willingness to apply the test of appropriateness to all aspects of an advertising program, i.e., does it work? Because advertising deals with subjective elements like words and visual images, it's very easy to let emotions gain the upper hand. Choices end up being made on the basis of the opinion—"I like it!"—rather than fact—"Let's test the ad's effectiveness in one market before we run it nationally."

Advertising gains in effectiveness when personal biases are eliminated. Decisions must be made on the basis of the appropriateness of the creativity, the budget, and the media to the task to be accomplished. This requires testing and a willingness to act upon the results of the tests.

Assign advertising responsibility to one person

Clearly defined authority is the key to an effective advertising program. Regardless of a firm's size, one person should be given clear authority and responsibility for creating, placing, and testing the firm's advertising. This person should also be responsible for informing all concerned parties—managers, department heads, field representatives, etc.—about upcoming advertisements.

In small firms, this advertising manager function can be a part-time function. In large firms, the advertising manager heads a staff of specialists.

Effective advertising cannot be created by a committee. This is because everyone is an "expert" in advertising; everybody has an opinion. People who would never presume to tell an electrical engineer which integrated circuit to use have no difficulty voicing their opinion on typefaces, headlines, or colors used in a firm's advertising.

This everybody-is-my-boss situation is fatal to creativity. Creative people have to receive instructions from one person and have their efforts evaluated by only one person. Otherwise, the copywriter, photographer, or artist will get hopelessly confused. At best, "lowest common denominator" advertising will result. At worst, money will be wasted and deadlines missed because different people gave different instructions. "Color? We took the pictures in black and white because Frank said it was going to be a black and white ad! What do you mean half-page horizontal? Bill told me half-page vertical!"

View advertising as a management function

Regardless of how large or small a business is, successful advertising is the result of the proper performance of four basic management functions. In a small business, all four would be performed by one person—the advertising manager. In a start-up situation, these might even be part-time functions. As a business grows, a staff is hired to help the advertising manager perform these functions.

What's important is not the number of hours or people devoted to performing the following four functions but that they be done, and that one person—the Advertising Manager—be held accountable for their proper execution.

1. Identify long-term objectives

A successful advertising program begins by asking, and answering, the questions: "Where are we now?" and "Where do we want to be?"

Research is often necessary to gain objective information at this point. "What do buyers of the product or service we're offering look for when they make their buying decision? What do prospective buyers of our product think about it? How does our product stack up against the competition? What sets our product apart from theirs?"

The goal is to identify a unique position for your product or service. All future advertising projects must contribute to achieving this position.

2. Define short-term goals and priorities

Next, it's important to define attainable short-term goals which will contribute to the long-term objectives. "What can we do today which will move us forward? What can we do next week? What's the first thing we should do? What should we do next? How soon?"

Hard choices and trade-offs will often have to be made, as there's never enough money to do everything. "If we advertise heavily on radio, there won't be enough money for newspaper! Are six full-color ads better than twelve black and white ads?

Here, again, the importance of a strong advertising manager becomes obvious. Compelling arguments can usually be made in support of both sides of an issue. An advertising committee could meet weekly for months and never come to a decision. A strong advertising manager with authority and confidence, however, would consider all the information available and make the best decision possible—and then move on towards creating the ads. A weak advertising manager, or committee, would become paralyzed by the choice, and nothing would get done.

3. Assemble resources

Next the advertising manager (and staff, if present) will gather together the tools and people necessary to create and place the ads in the appropriate media.

"What advertising agencies have experience in our field? Which agencies should we invite to give us a presentation? What copywriters, artists, and photographers are available? Which printers should we have bid on our work? Who's the best typesetter in town?"

Gathering resources also includes setting up an in-house information network. "Who has the information we need to complete our new product brochure? Who will take the time to explain the technical points to us in an understandable language?"

Strong advertising managers have many options available and the courage to try alternate ways of doing things. Weak advertising managers will do things the way they've always been done. Needless to say, the latter approach often increases costs (due to supplier complacency) and restricts creativity.

4. Schedule products

An advertising manager's most important job is to prepare a written advertising plan. This plan should start with a statement of the long-term objectives of the advertising program and detail the following information about each ad:

- Where it's going to run.
- When it's going to run (i.e., "Street Date").
- What size it's going to be.
- How much it's going to cost to prepare the ad.
- How much it's going to cost to run the ad.

Deadlines and responsibilities for each step in the creative process have to be spelled out in detail. "In order to meet the deadline, the printer has to have it in his hands by June third. In order for the printer to have it by June third, photographs have to be taken by May fifteenth. In order to take photographs by May fifteenth, Research and Development has to ship prototype samples by May first."

The advertising plan is a "living document"; it can be modified as conditions change. Non-performing media may be eliminated. Or the total budget may be modified to accommodate sales increases or decreases, or changes in a competitor's advertising expenditures.

But, regardless of how large or small an advertising budget is, your plan has to be reduced to a single written document which shows at a glance what's going to happen, when it's going to happen, and who's responsible.

Delegate creativity

Rarely can one person do everything. It's rare to find someone skilled with both words and visual images. It's virtually impossible to find an Advertising Manager who can write effective copy, prepare an attention-getting layout, specify typeface and type size, and then prepare camera-ready artwork.

It's even less likely that you'll find an advertising manager with the photographic or illustration skills required to create the firm's ads.

And even if such a master of all trades did exist, as a business grows, the research and planning functions quickly increase to a point where there's less and less time for the advertising manager to write copy or prepare camera-ready artwork.

Thus, the ability to effectively delegate creativity is required of even part-time advertising managers with small budgets.

Evaluate results

No one can predict how effectively an ad will perform before it runs. But ads can often be tested before major media investments are made. And after ads run, their

Figure 6.1

The Advertising Job Order

The key to successfully delegating creativity is to prepare written job orders for each project (no matter how small). These job orders should be prepared on multi-copy paper, so that everyone concerned can get a copy. This job order should identify project goals, budgets, and deadlines as specifically as possible.

"We need an ad for next Thursday!" is not a good way to delegate creativity. Much better is the job order specifying:

•Purpose of ad	"We want people currently buying our competition's paper cutter to buy ours instead."
•Preferred approach	"Show how we use carbon steel cutting blades instead of the plastic blades everyone else uses."
•Size of ad	"Two columns by six inches"
•Creative budget	"Keep it under $500, including typesetting."
•Deadline	"I need a rough layout in my hands by Monday, July eighteenth, and finished artwork by Friday, August first."

effectiveness can be monitored—so winners can be repeated and losers eliminated.

Many newspapers, for example, offer "split-run" testing. Split-run tests involve creating two versions of an ad, which appear in alternate copies of a newspaper. The ads are identical, except for the headline, illustration, or price being tested for effectiveness. A coded coupon, or other reader response device, is included. By comparing the number of version A coupons redeemed with the number of version B coupons redeemed, it's possible to identify the headline, illustration, or price with the strongest appeal.

The easiest way to gauge the effectiveness of your advertising is to simply note, on the advertising plan the sales or requests for information which resulted from each advertisement. After a while, definite patterns will appear which can be used to guide future decisions.

Action Plan For:
"Establishing an Advertising Structure"

❑ Learn what advertising can and cannot do.

❑ Be responsible in your advertising: Describe your product or services benefits simply, in terms the buyer can relate to; allocate sufficient resources to accomplish your advertising objectives.

❑ Delegate responsibility for your advertising program to one person, your advertising manager.

❑ Your advertising manager's job is to identify long-term objectives, define short-term priorities, assemble resources, schedule projects, and effectively delegate creativity.

❑ Test your ads and evaluate the results so winners can be repeated and losers eliminated.

Chapter Seven:

Choosing the Right Advertising Media

....

Successful advertising requires that the right advertising message be placed in the right media.

Creativity is wasted if your advertisement isn't read or seen or heard by prospective buyers of your product or service. The goal of successful media planning is to target your advertising dollars where those most likely to buy your product or service are concentrated.

This requires an awareness of the strengths and weaknesses of each alternative open to you and a willingness to test and experiment.

A full-service advertising agency provides expertise in planning, buying, and evaluating media options. But many smaller businesses are not able to afford this kind of service. Whether you are able to employ an agency or not, you should have a working knowledge of the basic media options open to you and an understanding of the basic techniques involved in making media decisions.

Understand your media options

Media options can be divided into print, broadcast, and direct mail.

Print

Print refers to either newspaper or magazine advertising. Print advertising is tangible—that's its main advantage. You can communicate a lot of detailed information. Readers can refer to your ad and reread what they missed the first time. Your ad can be clipped and filed for future reference. Coupons can be added.

Print advertising offers fairly accurate circulation information. The Audit Bureau of Circulation monitors the numbers of copies printed and mailed. This "guaranteed" circulation ensures that your ad will at least have a fighting chance to reach the prospects you're paying for. Whether the ad is read or not depends on you—and how well your creative people did their jobs.

Newspapers

Newspaper advertising runs the gamut from neighborhood weeklies to newspapers with strong regional, or even national readership. The larger metropolitan Sunday newspapers, like the *Boston Globe* or the *New York Times,* have an impact far beyond the borders of their home city. The *Wall Street Journal,* too, is more like a daily magazine than a newspaper in its nationwide impact.

A newspaper is a shopper's medium. Your ad is one of the reasons the newspaper was purchased in the first place. Studies have shown that readers prefer newspapers with ads to newspapers without ads.

Magazines

Magazine can be general (*Time, Newsweek*), special interest (*Stereo Review, Car & Driver, Wooden Boat*), regional (*Boston, Houston Home and Garden*), or trade (*Computer Retailing, Modern Materials Packaging*). Regional inserts in national magazines add further flexibility. These permit local advertisers to advertise in just those issues of *Time* and *Sports Illustrated* sent to subscribers in their area.

Magazines permit you to to target your market and do a better job of communicating than newspapers. Magazine readers generally pay to receive the magazines they get, so they're more likely to pay attention to the ads. In addition, since magazines are printed on better quality paper than newspapers, illustrations and photographs reproduce better.

Broadcast

Broadcast refers to radio and television advertising. These media offer you the ability to communicate quickly with great numbers of potential buyers of your product or service.

Radio

Radio advertising offers you an opportunity to target your advertising dollars to those markets most likely to buy from you. Each radio station is formatted to appeal to a distinct market segment. The music played, the personalities of the announcers, the way news is treated, and the overall tempo of the station all determine the type of listener who will tune in.

As a result, each station's listeners represent a unique combination of education, buying power, and lifestyle aspirations.

Radio is a universal medium. Most homes have more than one radio. Over ninety-five percent of all cars have radios. People wake up to radio, drive to radio, work to radio, and go to sleep to radio.

Television

Television offers the ability to add movement to your message. You can impact viewers three ways at once with your advertising message. You can talk to them, you can demonstrate your product or service, and you can superimpose important words (like prices or your name) over the image.

Television offers you the opportunity to communicate with a lot of people at once. Television is the primary at-home entertainment for most people. The average American spends more time watching than reading. Television is the way most people keep in touch with world events. And it is a tremendous credibility-builder for most advertisers. Prospects and customers think differently about your business when they see your advertisement on television.

Direct mail

Direct mail offers you an opportunity to target your advertising dollars to those most likely to buy from you. Prospective recipients of direct mail can be "hot" or "cold."

"Hot prospecting" refers to sending your advertising message to past customers or prospects to whom you tried to sell but didn't sell the first time around. "Cold prospecting" refers to purchasing or assembling the names and addresses of individuals or firms you've never dealt with but who are likely to be interested in your product or service.

Direct mail can be used to sell specific products by mail, or it can be used as a lead generator for later follow-up by your sales staff.

Like newspapers or magazines, direct mail advertising is tangible. Your message exists in black and white (or color) on paper. This means that a lot of information and details can be communicated. Readers can refer to your message to

Figure 7.1

Media Advantages and Disadvantages at a Glance

Media	Advantages	Disadvantages
Newspapers	• Your ad has size and shape, plus can be as large as necessary to communicate as much of a story as you care to tell.	• Clutter—your ad has to compete for attention against large ads run by supermarkets and department stores.
	• The distribution of your message can be limited to your geographic area.	• Poor photo reproduction limits creativity.
	• Split-run tests are available to test your copy and your offer.	• A price-oriented medium—most ads are for sales.
		• Short shelf life. The day after the newspaper appears, it's history.
	• Free help is usually available to create and produce your ad.	• Waste circulation. You're paying to send your message to a lot of people who will probably never be in the market to buy from you.
	• Fast closings. The ad you decide to run today can be in your customer's hands two days from now.	• A highly visible medium. Your competitors can quickly react to your prices.
Magazines	• High reader involvement means more attention will be paid to your advertisement.	• Long lead times (generally 90 days) means you have to make plans a long time in advance.
	• Less waste circulation. You can place your ads in magazines read primarily by buyers of your product or service.	• Higher space costs plus higher creative costs.

Media	Advantages	Disadvantages
Magazines	• Better quality paper permits better photo reproduction and full-color ads. • The smaller (generally 8 1/2 by 11 inch) page permits even small ads to stand out.	
Radio	• A universal medium—enjoyed at home, at work, and while driving. Most people listen to radio at one time or another during the day. • Permits you to target your advertising dollars to the market most likely to respond to your offer. • Permits you to create a personality for your business using only sound and voices. • Free creative help is usually available. • Rates can generally be negotiated. • Least inflated medium. During the past ten years, radio rates have gone up less than other media.	• Because radio listeners are spread over many stations, to totally saturate your market you have to advertise simultaneously on many stations. • Listeners cannot refer back to your ads to go over important points. • Ads are an interruption to the entertainment. Because of this, radio ads must be repeated to break through the listener's "tune-out" factor. • Radio is a background medium. Most listeners are doing something else while listening, which means your ad has to work hard to be listened to and understood. • Advertising costs are based on ratings which are approximations based on diaries kept in a relatively small fraction of a region's homes.

Media	Advantages	Disadvantages
Television	• Permits you to reach great numbers of people on a national or regional level.	• Ads on network affiliates are concentrated in local news broadcasts and on station breaks.
	• Independent stations and cable offer new opportunities to pinpoint local audiences.	• Creative and production costs can quickly mount up.
	• A medium that enhances a company's image.	• Preferred items are often sold out far in advance.
		• Most ads are ten or thirty seconds long, which limits the amount of information you can communicate.
Direct Mail	• Your advertising message is targeted to those most likely to buy your product or service.	• Long lead-times required for creative printing and mailing.
	• Your message can be as long as necessary to fully tell your story.	• Requires coordinating the services of many people: artists, photographers, printers, etc.
	• You have total control over all elements of creation and production.	• Each year over 20 percent of the population moves, meaning you must work hard to keep your mailing list up to date.
	• A "silent" medium. Your message is hidden from your competitors until it's too late for them to react.	• Likewise, a certain percentage of the names on a purchased mailing list is likely to be no longer useful.

review important points. Your message can be as large as necessary to communicate the details of your product or service. (This is in contrast to broadcast ads, which are usually restricted to ten, thirty, or sixty seconds.)

Decide on a strategy

One of the first decisions you have to make when choosing your media is to decide whether you want to use a "push" or a "pull" strategy.

A push strategy concentrates your advertising on the middlemen between you and your customers. In push strategies, for example, a lot of attention is often directed towards convincing retailers and distributors to stock and promote a product to customers and end-users. In this case, trade magazines might be extensively used.

A pull strategy emphasizes end-users. You create a demand for your product or service that the middlemen must satisfy, whether they want to or not.

Needless to say, the more you know about the dynamics of your business and your markets, the better job you'll do choosing the appropriate strategy. Whatever you choose, your strategy must be consistent with the rest of your marketing efforts and with your long-term business goals.

In most cases, by analyzing the buyers of your product or service, the types of media you should consider will become immediately apparent.

For example, if you're a manufacturer of display racks and fixtures for banks, newspaper and radio advertising will not be as effectively targeted as aiming your advertising at purchasing agents in the banking industry. Instead, advertising in trade magazines like *Bank Marketing* or *ABA Banking Journal* would get you more value for your advertising dollars.

Or, you might decide on a direct mail campaign to the appropriate group in the banking industry.

The difficulty, of course, is not so much in deciding the types of media where you should advertise (e.g., radio versus trade magazine) as making specific choices between the same types of media. After you've decided that trade magazines make the most sense for you, how do you choose between *Automotive Week* and *Automotive News*? On the local level, how do you decide on Radio Station A instead of Radio Station B?

That's where the importance of customer surveys and testing comes in.

Let your customers guide your decisions

There is a tremendous amount of insecurity involved in most media decisions. Often, media decisions involving hundreds of thousands of dollars are based on

---

Figure 7.2

Ten-Second Media Quiz

Please list the newspapers you read regularly:

	Daily	Sunday
First Choice	_____	_____
Second Choice	_____	_____
Third Choice	_____	_____

Please list the radio stations you listen to regularly:

First Choice _____

Second Choice _____

Third Choice _____

Fourth Choice _____

Fifth Choice _____

Have you recently seen or heard our advertising? _____

Where? _____

Thank you for your help!

Your logo

---

the promises of commissioned media sales representatives. Since the income of these sales representatives is proportionate to the amount of advertising they sell, they usually are not the best people to listen to when making your decision. If you work with an agency, they will take care of this sort of thing, of course.

Whether it's you or your agency making the decision, listen to your customers. Who knows more about the media preferences of your customers than your customers themselves?

Strong media planning begins with an organized survey sent to random samples of your present customers. "Organized" is the key word. Asking questions at a cocktail party or convention is not enough. You want your survey to be treated seriously by your customers, and you want the information gathered in a way which will permit careful analysis.

Your media preference survey can be sent to your present customers on your firm's letterhead, prefaced by a short covering letter, or you can have an independent testing firm prepare and mail the survey over their name. In either case, a

---

self-addressed, postage-paid envelope should be included to increase survey response.

See Figure 7.2, a ten-second media quiz, which you can use for your own media survey.

Your Media Preference Survey will serve two purposes. One is to ascertain the success of your current advertising. The other is to identify places where you should be advertising.

Questions like: "Where have you seen or heard our advertising?" will show you where your present advertising is succeeding. Questions like: "Which of the following magazines do you read on a regular basis?" or "Approximately how many hours a week do you watch (or listen to) the following stations?" will guide your investigations into new media options.

Figure 7.3

Testing: The Key to Better Media Decisions

One of the best ways to test the effectiveness of your various media alternatives, without spending great amounts of money, is to run a series of small teaser ads, which contain buried offers.

In the body copy of one ad, for example, you might invite readers to write Department A-101 for a free sample of your product or a free booklet describing how readers can save money while purchasing the type of product or service you sell. In another ad in a different medium, you might invite readers to write Department B-202 for the same offer.

A different number can be assigned to each medium where your ad is run.

By adding up the responses to these buried offers, you can easily gauge the effectiveness of each medium.

Evaluate results

When establishing a structure for your media purchases, it's important to set a structure for ongoing evaluation of the results of your advertising.

Ideally, the same advertisement should run in several different media, with careful records being kept of the results each time it is run. Coupons, requests for further information, or some other indicator of response can be used to gauge each ad's effectiveness. If identical ads are used in each medium, any differences in response can be directly traced to that medium.

It is important, of course, that the exact same ads be used in each medium if accurate results are to be achieved. If you change the headline, photograph, or price used in each advertisement, differences in response might be traceable to the headline, photograph, or price, instead of the media being tested.

Action Plan For:
"Choosing the Right Advertising Media"

❑ Gain an understanding of the strengths and weaknesses of print, broadcast, and direct mail media.

❑ Determine your strategy and establish a budget.

❑ Begin your media planning with an organized survey sent to random samples of your present customers.

❑ Keep careful records and evaluate the performance of each ad you run.

Chapter Eight:

Direct Mail Advertising

....

A strong direct mail program can be a tremendous asset to any growing business. Direct mail permits advertising messages to be communicated to potential buyers on a very cost-efficient basis.

Instead of diluting advertising funds by communicating with people who have no possible interest in your product or service (which happens when you advertise on the radio or in the newspaper), direct mail permits you to target your advertising dollars to those who are most likely to buy from you.

Choose the right format

There are many direct mail formats you can use. The format that's right for you will be determined by three factors:

- the complexity of the message you're delivering;
- the response you're trying to get from the reader; and
- your available budget resources.

The simpler your goals, the simpler your mailing. That's one of the beauties of direct mail—you can adapt it to your needs.

Organize the names

It's useful to view the recipients of your direct mail message as either "hot" prospects or "cold" prospects.

Figure 8.1

Ways That Direct Mail Can Help

Customer Reinforcement

Past customers can be converted into future customers by constantly reminding them of your existence, thanking them for their past patronage, and giving them more reasons to buy. A simple, sincere thank you letter to past customers immediately after their purchase creates a tremendous amount of good-will.

Building Referrals

Since most first-time buyers of any goods or services ask their friends for recommendations, anything you do to reinforce your past customers generates word-of-mouth recommendations.

Promotions

Direct mail can motivate customers to buy what you want to sell, when you want to sell it. Even service businesses can benefit from promotions which increase consumer demand.

New Product Introductions

Customers are always interested in what's new. People almost always read newsletters that describe new products or services or new applications of existing products or services. The pay-off comes in direct sales and good-will.

Lead Generation

If your business involves calling on customers and prospects, direct mail can increase the efficiency of those efforts by providing qualified leads. This saves you the trouble and expense of calling on the wrong people.

Customer Surveys

Surveys of past customers can provide you with good, solid information about your business, your competition, and your market. This translates into more effective advertising. Also, the very act of sending out a survey reinforces the professionalism of your business.

Direct Sales

Many products can be sold directly through the mail, eliminating the need for salespeople and retail space. Or allowing customers who can't come to your store to buy from home. Some people have made their fortunes this way, and many businesses have become more profitable through direct mail selling.

Organizing the names also involves a decision about who should maintain your mailing list. There are advantages and disadvantages to doing it yourself, but the same is true of lettershops, or fulfillment houses as they're sometimes called.

Figure 8.4 shows some of the ways you can maintain your list and what you should consider when making your decision. Generally, maintaining the list in-house is less expensive but more difficult and time-consuming. Lettershops tend to be more expensive but more convenient.

Determine the cost of your mailing

Regardless of the size of your mailing, it will consist of two categories of expenses: "creative" costs and "exposure" costs.

Creative costs are those involved in preparing your message, including:

- the time spent planning the mailing;
- the time spent writing the copy for the mailing;
- art costs—layout and design, typesetting, mechanical, and assembly; and
- photographic and illustration costs.

Exposure costs are those involved in delivering your message. These include:

- printing costs;
- mailing costs—list rental or list upkeep, addressing, zip code sorting and bundling, etc.; and
- postage costs.

Anything you do in-house will save you money, but you have to weigh the possible savings against the efficiency of a good outside service.

Keep in mind that there are different ways of accomplishing the same thing. For example, you might want to price out a mailing program using your own list maintenance facilities (e.g., hand-addressed envelopes) on a worksheet and compare it with the cost of having envelopes addressed by a lettershop. The worksheet makes for easy comparison.

Project returns: Will the mailing pay off?

A relatively simple formula will help you find the break-even point of a mailing, regardless of whether you're a book keeping service looking for additional clients, a hardware store planning a preferred customer sale, or a small publisher with a new book to offer. Here's the formula:

Total cost of the mailing + the average profit per sale = the sales that have to be made to cover the cost of the mailing.

This formula is a "true" formula because it takes into account the cost of providing the goods or services.

For example, look at the hardware store's preferred customer sale.

Cost of mailing (from the worksheet): $325.00
Average margin per sale
(based on experience of a $50.00 average
sale at 18 percent margin): $9.00

Number of customers needed at this sale 37

Figure 8.2

"Hot" and "Cold" Prospects: A Few Examples

Bookkeeping/Accounting Service

"Hot" prospects include past customers and people who have inquired about their services but decided either to do the work themselves or use another firm.

"Cold" prospects include small businesses in the area and, at tax time, everyone.

Hardware Store

"Hot" prospects include past customers, as well as people who visited the store on Arbor Day and entered the drawing for a free hedgeclipper.

"Cold" prospects include all homeowners in the area.

Advertising Agency

"Hot" prospects include people who have purchased advertising materials before and people who have called or written for more information.

"Cold" prospects include any retailers with an ad budget.

In other words, a 4 percent return is needed to justify the cost of the mailing. So, if four out of 100 people respond, the hardware store's preferred customer mailing will at least pay for itself. The question then becomes: Is it reasonable to expect four (or more) out of 100 people to buy?

Create the mailing

Volumes have been written on producing direct mail. The amount of information available is staggering, so we've included a brief bibliography of some of the better sources.

Suffice it to say that the available literature on the topic gets so detailed that you can actually point to the statistics which show that mailings with stamps applied at an angle produce better results than mailings with stamps squarely on the envelope!

For most small or mid-sized businesses, however, a few simple rules will greatly increase the effectiveness of even the simplest direct mailing. Here are some things to consider.

Selfishness: "What's in it for me?" is the attitude people will have when they receive your mailing. Unless you tell them, in no uncertain terms, exactly what is in it for them, they're not going to respond to your mailing. Chances are they won't even finish reading it.

A sale at a hardware store is not really important to people. But "homeowners interested in finishing off their basements," or "Saturday morning mechanics looking to save money on quality tools" would be interested.

Clarity: Your direct mail message has to be as brief and to the point as possible.

Benefits have to be stated in as few words as possible. The words have to be printed large enough so they can be easily read and there must be enough white space on the page so their meaning is available at a glance. The busy reader should be able to pick up your direct mail piece and instantly find out "What's in it for me?"

Figure 8.3

Direct Mail Formats

Postcards

Choose postcards when you want to communicate a simple idea at the lowest possible cost. They are quick and easy to prepare and can be dropped right in the mailbox.

They are ideal for retailers announcing special promotional events—a hardware store announcing a special Preferred Customer Sale, for example.

Personalized Letters

When a more sophisticated message must be conveyed to a smaller audience (often an audience known to the sender), a personalized letter can be the perfect choice.

With the current advances in word processing equipment, plus the competitiveness of lettershops and direct mail firms, personalized letters can be worth the money.

Self-mailers

Self-mailers are printed brochures sent without an envelope. A variety of sizes can be accommodated, including full-size catalogues with hundreds of pages. Newsletters announcing new products or services are the most appropriate uses for self-mailers. A single sheet of 11 by 17 inch paper folded in half creates four 8 1/2 by 11 pages: enough to cover almost any product or service in sufficient detail.

Since you only need to add address labels, self-mailers are a good choice for a large mailing. It would be the ideal format, for example, to promote a seminar on tax planning for business owners.

Mailing Packages

The above three formats are appropriate for mailing to customers or prospects in a specific area or region, since they're intended to bring people into your place of business.

You need a different technique for direct-response selling, i.e., selling a product to people you will never meet. In direct-response selling, you are trying to get people to send a check or credit card authorization through the mail. In this case, four-part direct mail packages are pretty standard. They usually include:

- a large envelope containing all the elements of the mailing;

- a printed cover letter which attempts to personalize the mailing and lead the reader to the brochure;

- a brochure describing the product;

- a response vehicle (usually a postage-paid envelope or business reply card).

A package this complete is rarely used by local businesses. It's overkill for the local merchant.

Simplicity: It should be easy for your reader to respond. It should be clear how a reservation can be made for the bookkeeping firm's tax planning seminar, for example.

Figure 8.4

Maintaining Your Mailing List

Format	Capacity	Advantages	Disadvantages
3x5 file cards or rotary file cards	Up to 500	Inexpensive Easy to check for duplicates Easy entry and removal	Entries have to be typed on envelope or address label each time mailing is made Best for first class mailings
Pressure-sensitive labels on office copier	Up to 1,000	Inexpensive Easy to add names	Hard to check for duplicates Hard to remove names Mailings have to be separately arranged in zip code order
Personal computer	Depends on the capabilities of your machine	Inexpensive to add names; easy to check for duplicates; computer performs other functions; prepares mailings in zip code order; entries in each zip code can be tallied to show where customers come from	Getting caught up with past customer names can often disrupt office routines; expensive equipment; requires planning to keep organized; address labels still have to be manually applied; time-consuming to delete returns after mailings; disgruntled employees can leave with print-out of customer list
Lettershops and mailing lists	Unlimited	Work performed without disrupting office routines: mailings go direct from printer to Post Office Lists safe from harm or theft	Expensive Many lettershops are only interested in large lists Less control over project Small clients sometimes put behind large clients, etc.

Test the mailing

Testing refers to a trial-and-error process of finding the appeal that will result in the greatest number of responses. The goal is to eliminate uncertainty and work toward predictability by testing the effectiveness of different headlines, prices, colors, or even mailing dates.

A successful testing program involves two prerequisites. Only one variable can be tested at a time, and careful records must be kept of responses.

Ideally, everything about the mailing should be the same, except the one variable being tested. Testing two prices on two dates would invalidate the test, because a reader might be responding to either the price or the date. (A direct mail offering on a Christmas crafts book would probably pull better in November than in April, regardless of the selling price.)

Even small business mailings can be coded, if the desire to test and improve direct mail efficiency is there.

Figure 8.5

Improving the Mailing

There are three ways to make your direct mail program more profitable.

1. Increase the profits per sale. This can be accomplished by either raising the selling price of the product or producing the product for less money.

2. Reduce the cost of the mailing. You can reduce the cost of the mailing by going to single-color printing instead of two-color, for example. You might want to consider a lighter paper stock for your brochure or mailing third class instead of first class.

3. Increase the efficiency of the mailing. If you can get a higher percentage of the people receiving your mailing to act, your profits will increase. More attention to creative aspects and testing will pay off.

All of the above can work together, of course. Ideally, through planning and hard work, you'll be able to increase profits per sale, reduce the cost of the mailing, and increase the effectiveness of your mailing. Small improvements in each area can add up to significantly increased profits.

For example, when mailing an invitation to a special sale you could print "Admission Tickets" in two colors. Simply adding up the "blues" and the "reds" would identify which list, price, headline, or other variable was more successful.

Over a period of time, by constantly eliminating the "losers" and building your mailings on "winning" appeals, you can format a direct mail program that will deliver predictable results—a program that will increase sales on a very cost-effective basis.

Figure 8.6

First Class Versus Third Class

Rate	Advantages	Disadvantages
First Class	Fastest possible mail delivery—usually overnight within same or adjacent zip codes. Requires no sorting or bundling of mail. Mail can be put in any box. Makes good impression. No minimum requirements. Fast delivery means your mailing will quickly begin to earn money for you. Zip codes preferable but not absolutely required. Undeliverables will be returned to you so you can delete them from your mailing list.	Highest possible cost per unit. Cost increases quickly as the weight of the mailing increases at one-ounce increments.
Presorted First Class	Most of the above benefits, plus you save several cents per piece for letters and one cent per piece on postcards. First class service, plus savings!	Minimum requirements: mailings must total at least 500 pieces, with minimum requirements per zip code. Requires annual pre sort fee. Check with your Post Office for current charges.
Third Class	Lowest possible cost per unit. Cost increases slowly as weight of mailing goes up.	Requires permit (check price). Mailings must be presorted and bundled by zip code. Longest delivery time of all. Lost revenues during delivery time.

Bibliography
Suggestions for Further Reading

Caples, John. *Tested Advertising Methods*. Englewood Cliffs, NJ, Prentice Hall. Single best guide to effective ad writing. Contains tried and proven rules for improving your creative abilities.

Kobs, Jim. *Profitable Direct Marketing*. Chicago, Crain Publications. Down-to-earth information about running your own direct marketing program, plus 11 detailed case studies.

Stone, Bob. *Successful Direct Marketing Methods*. Chicago, Crain Publications. The bible of direct marketing. Practical information on each page.

Direct Mail Advertising and Selling for Retailers. An anthology. National Retail Merchants Association, 100 West 31st Street, New York, NY 10001. 28 chapters with worksheets.

Hodgson, Richard (Ed.). *Direct Mail and Mail Order Handbook*. Chicago, Dartnell Corporation. 1,555 pages of information by various leaders in the field; incredibly detailed.

Figure 8.7

The Meaning of "Address Correction Requested"

"Address Correction Requested" on a piece of mail you receive in your mailbox means that the sender wants to keep track of you.

Mail is always forwarded for one year after a move, but the sender is not informed that the mail is being forwarded to a different address.

At the end of the year, mail will continue to be sent, yet destroyed after the forwarding order has expired.

"Address Correction Requested" means that the sender is willing to pay an additional 30 cents to find out your current address. First or third class mail will be forwarded to the newest address, and a copy of the old and new addresses will be sent to the original mailer, so your address can be updated.

Once or twice a year is usually enough to include "Address Correction Requested" on your mailings, to keep your list up to date.

Action Plan For:
"Direct Mail Advertising"

❑ Choose the direct mail format that's appropriate to your needs.

❑ Build your list of names from "hot" and "cold" prospects, and decide how you'll maintain your list.

❑ Determine both the creative and exposure costs of your mailing.

❑ Find the break-even cost of your mailing and project the return needed to cover the mailing's cost.

❑ Create and test the mailing, one variable at a time. Improve your mailings over time.

Chapter Nine:

Prospect-Centered Selling

....

Advertising is one way to make many people aware of the benefits of your products and services. But sales aren't necessarily made because a person read, saw, or heard your ad. Often it's direct one-on-one efforts that produce the actual cash in hand. That's why prospect-centered selling is a valuable tool for every business.

Prospecting has been defined as "searching for something of value." In gold prospecting, you head for an area where there are known gold deposits. You search for the deposits of black sand, shovel some into your pan and begin to discard the black. What remains is the thing of value—the gold. In sales prospecting, the objective is to uncover the sale. The role of the salesperson is to persuade the prospect to purchase the goods or service using techniques that put the prospect's interest first.

Yet despite the importance of persuasion in sales, some observers say only five percent of sales personnel are "persuaders." Ninety percent are considered "order takers"—the sellers who do not increase sales volume by generating new business, but simply take orders. Another five percent could be called "charlatans." These salespersons are characterized by the fast-talking, hard-selling approach.

The persuaders, those who make people aware of their needs and demonstrate how the company's product or service satisfies those needs, are the top sellers in any organization. The techniques they use are the ones detailed here.

Project a positive attitude

Become comfortable with yourself as a salesperson. Despite open prejudices to the contrary, selling is an excellent career. It can be fun and satisfying, and for the independent business owner, sales skills are vital.

Your attitude or your posture toward yourself and your product are communicated in a variety of ways. Words, tone, the way you dress, body language, the way you talk about your competition, eye contact, and scores of other indicators let your prospect know your true feelings. A positive attitude is contagious. It prepares your prospect for the best from you and your product.

A successful insurance salesman recalls that he never sold insurance to anyone until he bought a policy for himself. Before that time, he was going through the motions. After that time, his sales pitch was the communication of a sincere belief in the importance of his product.

Qualify your prospects

Who needs your product? Who can pay for it? Is that person a decision maker? A qualified prospect is a person who has a need that you can satisfy, is able to afford the product, and has the authority to buy. The persuader, that successful seller described above, will devote 30 to 60 percent of his or her efforts to prospecting. The vast majority of salespeople spend far less.

How do you find leads that can develop into qualified prospects? Among the ways are: advertising, direct mail, cold calls, examining previous sales records and door-to-door canvassing. Once identified, these prospects must be qualified. Some, such as present customers, are already qualified. For the others, you must obtain information on the prospect's income, interests, problems and authority to purchase. In some cases it will be possible to investigate before the call by talking with a potential buyer's friends, business associates or customers. In other instances it may be necessary to qualify on the spot. That is, you will have to ask questions. What type of work do you do? What is your biggest problem in running this business? Are you the manager in charge

---

Figure 9.1

Sources of Sales Leads

Current customers
Advertising
Previous sales records
Telephone calls
Marketing efforts
Door-to-door canvassing
Sales calls
Public relations
Associations
Direct mail
Your suppliers
The competition
Exhibits and conventions
Service and credit departments
Cold calls
Referrals

---

of decisions regarding purchases of this kind? If you have gained the prospect's respect and have shown genuine interest, your questions will be answered.

Cultivate a successful approach

If your prospect is answering your questions, you are already well into your approach—gaining the qualified prospect's attention and establishing levels of trust and respect. A successful approach gives you the opportunity to demonstrate and close. A poor approach sends you back to the bench no matter how desirable your product or service.

It has been said that based on your approach the prospect will, in 30 seconds or less, decide whether you can be trusted and are of interest. Factors influencing that decision include your appearance, the words you say, your body language, and the kind of energy you generate. Of primary importance to the success of your approach is the degree to which you are comfortable with it. Self-knowledge, in sales as in other areas, comes from experience. Consider these approaches, bearing in mind that each must be adapted to your prospect and to your product.

- *Show personal interest.* Cite an advertisement or a newspaper article about your prospect. "I read recently that you are opening a branch in the West County area."
- *Deliver something.* Premiums are welcome. "Our company is sponsoring a tax seminar next month on the new tax law changes. This certificate entitles you to free admission."
- *Hand over the product.* Have you ever refused to take something when it was handed to you? Most of us haven't. Ideally, you will be able to hand your prospect the actual product. If it is too big (an automobile) or too intangible (a service), consider giving a recent annual report, a package of materials describing what your company does, or a model of the large product, such as a miniature car.
- *Make a claim.* Focus it and make it true. "Our experience with other new businesses has given us an edge on helping clients avoid start-up errors."
- *Tell a story.* When the voice of experience talks, prospects listen. "We helped a company like yours save more than 50 hours of annoying, costly paperwork each month with a simple computer hook up."
- *Make an offer.* An introductory offer can move a prospect. "Our hottest prospects routinely receive a month of free record-keeping services."
- *Show the benefits.* "We can do three things for you: save you money in taxes, eliminate unnecessary book work, and guide you through complicated federal regulations."

- *Offer help.* "I came to meet with you today because my calculations indicate that our firm could save you 40 hours of work each week; that's thousands of dollars over a year's time."
- *Solve a problem.* Your investigative homework should reveal specific problems faced by your prospect. Suggest a variety of good solutions. These need not have anything to do with your product or service. The goal is to get you in to see the prospect under favorable conditions.

In considering these or any other approaches, remember that people make purchase decisions; corporations do not. There is no universally successful approach. Yours must fit you and the prospect. The time it will take to select and hone your approach will pay off in the end. If you can become aware of your prospect's perceptions of his or her own needs and how your product can solve perceived problems, you're way out in front.

Demonstrate the benefits of your product or service

A good demonstration does two things for you. It educates your prospect in the uses of your product, and it gives you a chance to understand your prospect better, opening the door for future sales. The key to your success in this area, as in all areas of selling, is planning.

Planning calls upon your experience and education about your product and your prospect. By becoming aware of what happens and what is likely to happen, you can effectively plan solutions in advance. This keeps you one step ahead of your prospect and any objections likely to emerge. Your planning strategy should include these steps:

- *Determine your objective.* Whether you are looking for a sale, or whether you are making an introductory visit to set the stage for further negotiations, know why you are there. If you are a sales manager, it is likely that you know what your sales force is trying to accomplish. But do they? Are they making sales calls with the objective of getting prospects to like them, or are they really trying to move the product?
- *Listen to your prospect.* If you let your prospect do the initial talking, you will gain a surprising amount of useful information. In fact, the prospect may even tell you how to make the sale. Many sales are killed by overtalkative salespeople who fail to listen. Often, prospects will talk themselves into a purchase.
- *Make a practice run.* Don't be afraid to try out your presentation. Rehearse it mentally; try it out on a friend or on videotape. Don't be afraid to incorporate a canned presentation into your pitch. Everyone needs something basic and dependable—a point of departure—that can be tailored to fit the needs of the individual prospect.

- *Segment your demonstration.* Start by listening and becoming familiar with all the key applications of your product. Many products or services can be offered singly or as a package. This permits you to meet the needs of the prospect for whom a limited amount is inadequate, as well as the prospect who considers your whole package too expensive.

When all is said and done, it is the degree to which you are prepared that will determine the success of your demonstration. Put yourself in the driver's seat; know your direction, but be prepared to alter your course along the way.

Meet objections

Objections are road signs to concluding a successful sale. By eliciting and disarming the prospect's objections, you move closer to your destination. The prospect who nods agreement to everything you say will not say yes in the end. The prospect who raises thoughtful questions is much more likely to become a client.

Meet objections with prepared responses; they will not threaten you if you have considered them in advance. When faced with an objection:

- *Welcome it.* "Thanks for pointing that out. It shows you really understand how much you stand to lose without a professional hand to guide you through the tax law changes." A positive, welcoming approach to objections puts you and the prospect on equal footing. If you try to rebut the objections, you become your prospect's adversary. Defensive behavior does not encourage sales. An objection means that the prospect is asking you to clear roadblocks to a purchase.
- *Get the prospect to say more.* Probe the objection; this gets the prospect talking and often results in the prospect selling him- or herself. "Tell me more about your feeling that a professionally designed interior will turn away some of your oldest and best customers." As the prospect talks, it may become clear that the stated objection is not the true objection standing between you and a sale. The real objection will likely be one you have prepared for and will have no trouble answering.
- *Choose from three options.* Answer the objection, ignore it, or close on it. If the objection is real in the mind of the prospect, you will know how to counter it. If it is a stall ("I'll have to talk this one over with my manager"), ignore it. Often, an objection leads to a close. A prospect suggests that it's too late in the tax year to benefit from the services of your company. "That's exactly why you should sign on with us today. You'll have your first report by the 20th of the month, and I'll be glad to file an extension for you immediately. Or, we can put you on the end of the month cycle." Again, tailor your response to what you know about your

prospect; you'll close on more sales that way. Adequate preparation will give you the confidence and the answers you need to disarm your prospect.

Close—gain the order

Remember the order takers? They don't persuade and they never try to close. They stop selling after they've made their demonstration, waiting for the prospect to demand the product or service. It doesn't work. Statistics indicate that the average sale is made on the fifth close. Good salespeople are not intimidated by a prospect who turns down a close. They're prepared with the next one, convinced that sooner or later the prospect will become a client.

Make it easy for the prospect to make a decision; it's hard for most people to make decisions readily. Your skill in facilitating a decision will result in a quicker close.

There is no single best time to close. Anytime your prospect is ready to commit is the right time to sign. Study your prospect to know when the iron is hot—then strike. The proper close is the one that makes your prospect into a client.

Consider the following closes. Remember that in prospect-centered selling the prospect's needs ultimately will determine your method.

- *Assumption close.* This is the basic close, where you assume the prospect wants your product. Fill in the order sheet as you go along. If no one stops you along the way, you've made a sale.
- *Direct close.* When everything has gone well, you may be able to ask your prospect a direct question: "When should we deliver the computer and software package, Ms. Duke?"
- *Summary close.* To lead a prospect to a decision, summarize the points you've made during your demonstration. "Just to clarify this in my own mind, was it our staff or our delivery system that you wanted more information about?"
- *Final objection close.* This close is beneficial when you find yourself in a ping pong game with a prospect: objection/answer, objection/answer. It commits the prospect to purchase once one last objection is resolved. Listen fully to the objection and the prospect's expanded reason. Agree that it is a significant problem and ask for confirmation that it is the only deterrent to ordering now. Then, seek agreement that once that problem is resolved, the sale is made. Answer the objection; it is likely that your prospect will not retreat into the objection/answer game. Write up the order.

Follow-up

Don't rest on your laurels. Selling doesn't stop once the order is written. Profitable repeat business depends on follow-up. And, like the prospect-centered sale, prospect-centered follow-up means that your prospect benefits from a follow-up tailored to his or her interest. Developing and following through on a good follow-up is just good business. Here's why:

- *It will keep your customer satisfied.* (Remember, he or she was just a prospect when you started this process!) And a satisfied customer can bring repeat business, referrals and word-of-mouth advertising, perhaps the most effective and the most cost-effective kind.

- *It will bring you additional prospects.* It has been demonstrated that often, following a successful sale, a satisfied customer will provide leads if asked. The fact that you turned a prospect into a customer means that there is a level of trust and understanding between you. If the customer trusts you with his or her own business, it is likely that he or she will want to spread that trust to colleagues and business associates.

- *It will permit you to sell other products.* The best time to sell more goods or services to a new customer is immediately after closing an initial sale. Again, the trust you've established carries plenty of clout. Use it.

- *It lets you know if your claims and promises made to the prospect about your product are being realized.* This kind of feedback can be of great benefit to you and your company. Follow-up is more than a "Hello, how's it going?" and a handshake. Your sincere interest in the performance of your product or the benefit realized from your service communicates a great deal about your belief in it and in yourself. As well, the information you gather can be used to improve the product—a ready form of market analysis.

The forms your follow-up can take are as varied as your customers. A follow-up can be a phone call, a visit, a tour of your plant or operation, an article on a subject you think the customer would be interested in, or, that old standby your mother insisted on, the thank-you note.

If your company conducts market research or product satisfaction polls, the information you learn from them could also be useful in a follow-up communication: "Dear Mr. Roberts: I wanted to share with you some data gathered from a recent market research effort on behalf of the 700 series. You may be interested to learn that the majority of those who bought 700s were like yourself, small business owners buying their first high-quality printer. We also learned that most of the customers found the instruction manual far too complex. To remedy that, we've prepared a new manual which should be off the press in four to six weeks. If you have had any difficulty with the old manual, or have any questions at all about your 700, I hope you'll feel free to call me anytime."

Sales are made to people, not organizations or boards of directors or institutions. And because it is people to whom we sell, support and reinforcement are of great importance. Everyone wants to feel that someone cares about their satisfaction with a purchase. A follow-up can do that and more.

The benefits of prospect-centered selling

Prospect-centered selling puts the prospect's needs first. It is, therefore, a technique that demands much more of the salesperson than the shotgun approach or any other method where knowledge of the prospect is not emphasized. Prospect-centered selling may not be the easiest method. Learning about your prospect, tailoring an approach, demonstration, close, and follow-up to his or her special needs requires thought and effort. But while the order taker and the charlatan may make the first sale, or even a repeat sale, somewhat easily, it's the persuader whose effectiveness can be judged over the long term. Time and effort are the investments; profitable sales are the return. Planning, preparing, listening, and persisting take time. Persuaders recognize the value of that input. The sale that is made on the basis of the prospect's best interests and concerns is more likely to be solid and more likely to lead to a lasting relationship than the sale built on luck, conniving or misinformation. Become a persuader, and, like the prospector with the pan sifting through black sand, go for the gold.

Checklist for success

✓ Have you arranged to see a decision-maker—the person with the authority to buy from you?

✓ Have you made an appointment and confirmed your appointment?

✓ Have you researched the prospect's needs? Can this call help you gather information?

✓ Review what you know about the prospect. What more do you need to know?

✓ What are the prospect's chief concerns? Are you prepared to address them?

✓ Review key points that you plan to make. How do you plan to make them?

✓ Do you have the necessary sales aids (charts, audio-visuals, displays, testimonials) suited to this particular prospect?

✓ What questions can you anticipate on the part of your prospect?

✓ Have you used positive words and images to persuade your prospect?

✓ What objections are likely to arise? How will you counter them?

✓ Can you find ways to permit the prospect to hold, feel, taste, or imagine using your product or service?

✓ Are there similarities between this prospect and others you have encountered? Can you use that knowledge to avoid pitfalls and roadblocks that beset you in the past?

✓ How will you follow up?

Action Plan For:
"Prospect-Centered Selling"

❏ Project a positive attitude toward yourself and your product.

❏ Find leads from a variety of sources and make sure to qualify your prospects.

❏ An approach that leads to a sale is one that puts your prospect's needs first.

❏ Carefully plan the sales presentation you'll make.

❏ Meet objections with prepared responses.

❏ Consider a variety of closes, and use the one that works best for your particular prospect.

Chapter Ten:

The Sales Manager

....

P rospect-centered selling is a valuable tool for building a company's customer base. Another way to develop new business is by delegating the entire function to one person: a sales manager.

Sales managers aren't just for large companies. Depending on your situation, hiring a sales manager may be the way to take advantage of opportunities for growth. But the main question to ask when you hire new help, make a substantial outlay for equipment, or consider any major expenditure, is how will this person/machine/ expense pay for itself in savings or increased sales? This topic raises some questions that will help you determine whether a sales manager could contribute to your company's growth.

When to hire

How do you determine whether a sales manager is necessary in a smaller company? Can a growing company afford a sales manager? When should you consider hiring a sales manager?

Thinking through a sales manager's potential job description will provide constructive ideas, regardless of immediate circumstances. Try this: If you had all the time in the world to devote strictly to selling or managing your sales force, what would your highest priorities be?

Or, if you didn't have to worry about selling, what would your five highest priorities be? Maybe you don't spend enough time planning, directing, and organizing because you're responsible for bringing in new business, too. The workload can be overburdening. As one owner put it, "From the time I get to my office until I leave, between phone calls, mail, and interruptions, I can't get anything done."

Usually, it would seem to be an issue of what the business can afford. But is it really? Taking on a sales manager is an investment in marketing management. Isn't the real issue, "What can I reasonably expect in increased sales?"

With the right person, the owner acquires a non-owner partner who can help to develop business strategy, structure the marketing function, and increase sales. The owner is relieved of many of the details of selling. (See the list of duties on page 103.) And while you may want to retain certain customers for personal attention, others can be serviced by a sales manager who knows that his or her income will derive from performance on these accounts.

A second practical occasion for establishing the position comes along when a company reaches a certain level of sales volume or number of salespeople to be managed. In the under $5 million sales volume category, a rule of thumb would be to allow three percent for sales management. This does not suggest that the sales manager is on a straight commission arrangement (see the Rewarding and Retaining section). But if you hope to attract competent sales management talent, you should probably plan on providing incentive up to approximately three percent of volume.

In addition to the sales volume figures, how many salespeople are to be managed? Salespeople cannot be trained, motivated, monitored, and controlled through bulletins, forms, and statistics. If your sales force is growing, you'll need a sales manager to provide direction and coherence. Whatever your situation, appointing a sales manager involves delegating authority. Less than this means that your time and effort will continue to be diverted.

Selection

You are looking for a person with outstanding management and sales skills. The person's methods and progress should be well-documented over a period of time. Obviously you'd want a management person clearly capable of achieving higher levels of gross volume and profits.

Many owners appoint sales managers from within the company—a top salesperson or an administrative person close to the owner, for example. Such promotions may be honestly earned. Yet, you must evaluate objectively whether the "logical" person would, in fact, be strongest for the development of the organization.

When business objectives are clear, characteristics and business background of the ideal candidate are more readily apparent. If a strong administrator is needed, promoting the outstanding salesperson from within can be dangerous. On the other hand, promoting a capable administrator into a position where new accounts, methods, and style are needed can be equally frustrating.

Whether you select a person from the same industry or an outstanding person from another industry, the ideal person will have contacts from your industry or another industry that will benefit your organization.

If you are considering hiring a sales manager, you are well advised to begin advertising well before you are ready to hire. Advertising and recruiting well ahead of time will give you a reading on available talent, potential costs of the investment, and potential gain. The ads, under a box number, should describe the size of the company, general area of activity (consumer goods, industrial, services), authority and responsibilities. A well-written ad in a prominent newspaper will bring many responses. Often, proven executives in large organizations seek new challenges and greater growth potential with a smaller organization.

Using a search firm to assist in the selection process is no different from taking on a specialist in any other area of business. Some are "head hunters" pure and simple; others are more skilled in understanding the client's needs and preferences.

Acquiring talented people is part of an owner's ongoing awareness of trends and developments in business. The best sources for sales manager prospects are within an owner's expanded circle of business contacts. Trade journal people (editors, publishers, representatives) are extremely knowledgeable and will do everything possible to aid members of their industries. This is also true of trade associations.

Other contacts are also important: suppliers, customers, friends in the trade. Confidentiality is vital. Owners should not allow themselves to be besieged with prospects. Simply letting a few contacts know that you are interested in talking with outstanding people will suffice to attract capable candidates.

Setting goals

By setting specific goals, owners are better able to direct their companies and generate stronger employee contributions. This gives employees a sense of achievement rather than simply performing at levels that enable them to hold jobs. Objectives may be stated in terms of time (by month, season, or year), product lines offered, areas covered, volume expectancy, profit structures, or some combination of these.

Figure 10.1

An Overview in Light of Your Marketing Plan

These questions will help you review and update your marketing priorities. These are important considerations in determining your need (or future need) for greater sales support.

1. What are your marketing goals for the next year in the following areas? The next five years? ☐ dollar sales ☐ unit sales ☐ profits ☐ market share ☐ activities to begin ☐ activities to stop ☐ customers to drop ☐ markets to enter ☐ markets to abandon ☐ customer base expansion ☐ market expansion ☐ production/product improvement ☐ reputation

2. Rank your principal marketing problems in order of urgency. _____

---

3. What major threats and what major opportunities does your company face in the next five years in the following areas? ☐ product and services ☐ competitive activity ☐ customer attitudes ☐ general business environment

4 What new competition do you expect in the next five years? _____

---

5. What competition do you expect will decline or disappear within the next year? Five years? Why? _____

---

6. How do your competitors structure their sales effort? _____

---

7. What proportion of your sales five years hence will come from new products? New markets? _____

Owners tend to know the sales volume and corresponding earnings needed to maintain the business, but too often, goals are only expressed in general terms. The strategy that emerges from undefined goals is "Get orders." Salespeople in such circumstances do not have strong direction and rely mainly on personal sales ability to glean a share of the business. Goals should be an integral part of the sales manager's job description and ongoing performance evaluation. The trick is to make goals ambitious but still realistic.

But in order to set goals for your sales manager, you must review your marketing plan. See Figure 10.1. What are your marketing strategies? Chances are, prospective customers can buy your products or services from more than one source. Will they buy from you because you are the biggest, smallest, nicest, most forthright, most reliable? Can you show important benefits more capably than your competitors? What are those benefits and how do you train your salespeople to communicate them? These will be central to the sales manager's job.

Many businesses forecast volume expectancy based on the previous year's sales rather than on genuine sales opportunities. In a newly created position, the competent sales manager knows that previous sales volume figures are only a starting point and will be able to set realistic goals for future sales. If such data is not available, the sales manager must devise methods for interpreting accounting and production records into sales analysis form.

Authority and methods

A sales manager's effectiveness evolves out of far more than personal ability. Assigned duties, delegated authority, and organizational tools must combine to reinforce the sales manager's position. In the first year, the cost of a new sales manager's position should be absorbed in redirection of the sales thrust, increased volume, new accounts, and revised territories.

In a typical situation, the owner will have brought in the major accounts. As is frequently the case, 80 to 90 percent of sales volume will come from 10 to 20 percent of all accounts. Even assuming that the owner will continue servicing a few of the major accounts, there will be sufficient prospects for the sales manager to earn his or her keep.

Figure 10.2

A List of Duties Common to the Position of Sales Manager

- Plan sales strategy.
- Budget the sales function.
- Hire, train, and motivate salespeople.
- Terminate unproductive salespeople.
- Monitor training progress in each territory.
- Monitor sales progress of each salesperson.
- Monitor activities of major accounts.
- Monitor product movement through territories.
- Evaluate salespeople's performance as to company objectives.
- Plan special promotions, contests, etc.
- Work with salespeople in the field.

- Plan, promote, and participate in trade shows.
- Develop major accounts.
- Service house accounts.
- Gather data on competition.
- Report periodically to top management.
- Expand territories under poor economic conditions; split territories under upswinging conditions.
- Create publicity for the sales function.
- Participate in trade association activities.
- Research new products.
- Conduct sales meetings.

The sales manager should chart, for periodic review, the level of sales over a given period of time. In most cases this will help show where sales increases can be expected and why. Each account is analytically reviewed as to potential, time allocation, and specifics of getting a greater share of business. He or she should also review sales techniques and frequency of calls.

Competent sales managers can schedule their time and energies in a manner that brings maximum returns. Researching new product ideas and gathering data on competition are ongoing functions of coordination between contacts, customers, and operations. To handle all duties efficiently, the sales manager may need access to a competent assistant, for example, a sales trainee, administrative person, or executive secretary capable of researching, analyzing, and communicating.

Rewarding and retaining

The nature of sales compensation allows small businesses to compete successfully against organizations many times their size. Compensation for sales performance, more than any other activity in an organization, is based on percentages, as Figure 10.3 shows.

The sales manager responsible for substantial increases in sales volume feels that income should keep pace. A sales manager on a base salary with expenses and an indefinite year-end bonus based on performance lacks specific incentive.

How should compensation be set up? You have a variety of options. By allocating a sales budget, sales managers accept the responsibility of motivating salespeople and managing in a manner that will bring maximum results for the company. In cases where the sales manager covers a territory or services key accounts, it is not unusual that the sales manager's compensation is offset by sales volume that would otherwise be commissionable or by paying a salaried salesperson. Owners should recognize this in planning the sales manager's compensation package.

At least two aspects of retaining a sales manager should be examined closely by owners: first, rewards in keeping with performance, and second, the consequences of losing an outstanding person to a bigger job, or worse, to a competitor.

Successful sales managers usually receive offers, whether they are sought or not, of more money than they are getting. In such cases the lure is greater immediate income plus other advantages that may include a promise of partnership, stock options, or other measurable gain.

The most effective insurance for owners is through developing commitment to the organization. Where key personnel share the goals of a team effort, they identify with it. The advantages of genuine work satisfaction and the feeling of belonging are powerful incentives for people. The many options available to owners in

Figure 10.3

Sales Compensation Figures Related to Volume of Sales

The chart below represents common sales compensation figures. However, what might be typical for one business could be totally inappropriate for another. Every business is unique, and factors such as size, nature of business, and location are important considerations in determining compensation.

At $5 million and above gross volume the sales manager has little time to service accounts personally. He or she will need an assistant(s) in handling the position. Note that only in the $5 million and above categories are stock options generally offered.

The most significant factor of stock options is that most major organizations adopted this management policy to achieve substantial growth. Stock may be given as part of the bonus, shares for reaching preset goals, or management may set up "insiders" price per share when goals are reached. The controlling factor is not the amount given; it is minimizing the tax consequences and providing motivation.

Stock options can be a more powerful tool to companies under the $5 million category. In higher volume companies, executives can more readily sell off shares if they want to move to another company. In small companies (fewer shares), stock ownership creates strong motivation to stay and build. Owners work out programs with the aid of accountants and attorneys.

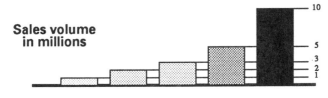

Sales volume in millions

Sales Volume (millions)	$1	$2	$3	$4	$5
Sales Budget (Sales Managers/Salespeople)	8%	8%	7.75%	7.25%	6.5%[1]
Sales Commission	7%	7%	7%	6%	5%
Sales Manager Packages					
Base Pay	$22,000	$26,000	$32,000	$43,000	$73,000
Expenses	4,000	4,500	5,500	7,000	12,000[2]
Bonus, Commission	6,000	6,000	9,000	12,000	15,000
Retirement	2,500	3,000	3,500	5,500	9,000
Totals	$34,500	$39,500	$50,000	$67,000	$109,000

[1] Actual costs will be hgher due to support staff these volume categories entail
[2] Stock options included

compensating and retaining key personnel are related to the long-term objectives of the company.

If you should lose a sales manager, a "campaign" is needed to fill the sudden void. Candidness with customers and salespeople will reflect confidence and assurance. Generally, customers buy from the company, not because of a person. The campaign might include a repeat of a special offered earlier. Whether the sales manager is replaced or other arrangements are made (an assistant takes over), emphasis must be placed on maintaining a high standard of performance.

Small business owners can learn from major organizations in the area of developing executive "packages" that encourage outstanding people to build careers on performance and tenure. Legal and accounting firms have hundreds of partners within a corporate structure. Executives in major corporations are indoctrinated into structures designed to retain them until retirement.

Your challenge lies in the definition that business management is the art of getting things done through people.

Action Plan For:
"The Sales Manager"

❑ Determine whether your company truly needs to have a sales manager by asking: What level of increased sales can be reached as a result?

❑ Select a person with a management background who has a proven track record for achieving higher levels of gross volume and profits.

❑ Begin advertising well before you're ready to hire.

❑ Review your marketing plan and set goals for your sales manager.

❑ Assign duties, delegate authority and provide organizational tools that reinforce the sales manager's position.

❑ Reward your sales manager in such a way that you encourage long-term commitment to your organization.

Chapter Eleven:

Break-even Analysis

....

A sales manager and a well-trained, motivated support staff can work wonders for increasing a company's income. But in order to map out their action plan, they need to know what's expected of them. You can help by quantifying their goals in realistic, workable terms—and by using break-even analysis.

Break-even analysis is a simple but powerful analytical tool which allows you to estimate the level of sales needed under current conditions for your business to break even. From that starting point, a whole host of other questions can be examined. There is no business, going or contemplated, which would not benefit from some application of this technique.

Break-even analysis is based on the proposition that the costs of doing business can be divided into the two broad categories of "fixed costs" and "variable costs," in relation to the volume of sales. All of the ensuing steps build from that proposition.

Divide costs into fixed and variable

Fixed and variable costs are not defined by a rigid list or set of rules but are defined, at least in part, by the context of your business at a given time under a reasonably constant set of conditions.

Within some reasonable range, fixed costs will not vary as sales go up or down. Examples are office rent, interest payments on loans, or office salaries.

Again, within some reasonable range, variable costs are directly associated with the volume of sales and go up as sales rise and fall as sales decline. The prime example is the actual cost of merchandise to the merchant who buys and then sells it or the cost of the materials that go into the plumber's helpers that Unstop, Inc. manufactures and sells.

But do not make the mistake of thinking that fixed and variable costs are the same as costs over which you have no control on the one hand and which you can control on the other.

The egg farmer has no control over the cost of the grain he feeds his chickens, yet that cost in total is directly variable with the number of chickens he feeds and thus the number of eggs he has available for sale. By the same token, you can often negotiate the size of the loan you receive, but once the loan is granted, the interest payments are essentially fixed no matter what sales level is achieved.

Do not assume that because the cost of goods, or some other expense, is commonly treated as a variable cost in break-even analysis, it should be treated as such in your business. The importer of high-fashion clothes places an order for so many garments, pays for them, and that is it. No matter how many are sold, the cost of the goods is fixed. Granted, the cost per garment sold will vary, but no one facing an importer who bought 20,000, sold five, and threw away the rest will argue that his cost of goods sold was variable.

The criterion here is reasonable: Costs which are variable for one business will be fixed for another and vice versa. Your particular set of conditions will be a factor in your decision to allocate costs to one category rather than another. Be reasonable, use your head—and you won't go far wrong. Don't refuse to use break-even analysis because you can't decide where to place one or two minor costs. That's not being reasonable.

The first aim in break-even analysis is to divide the costs of your business into the two broad categories of fixed and variable.

The reasoning is simple. For every dollar of sales, a certain, directly-tied cost will be incurred. This is the variable cost. Left over, after that cost has been incurred, will be something to apply to the fixed costs which are there no matter what the volume of sales may be. When enough sales dollars are realized so that the leftovers equal the fixed costs, the sales break-even point has been reached. The business is neither making nor losing money.

Allocate semi-variable costs

Immediately, someone will point out that the real world is not so simple and that many costs are not directly tied to the volume of sales but are not truly fixed either.

Some people try to break such costs down into fixed and variable components— the basic monthly charge on a telephone versus the long distance toll calls that are directly tied to sales. Some try to devise elaborate formulas for allocation based on everything from past experience to the star charts of the astrologer.

Such contortions are caused by losing sight of the fact that whichever category costs are allocated to, the break-even point remains the same because break-even occurs when total costs equal total revenues.

In most cases, experience has shown that for the first cut, either of two methods works perfectly well.

Relate costs to sales for the period

To calculate break-even sales volume, three numbers from the same time period are required. These are total fixed costs, total variable costs, and total sales associated with those costs. Note that these do not have to be real, historic figures—they can be forecasts. These three numbers are inserted into a simple mathematical formula to calculate the break-even volume.

You should pay particular attention to the implications of the phrase "associated with those costs," as the usefulness of break-even analysis always rests on your costs. The more detailed your financial reports, the more applications of break-even to your profit can be made. One good example is the restaurant owner who has both a food and a liquor operation in separate parts of the restaurant, but cannot say how much he makes from one or the other. Yet they are very distinct kinds of operations, so distinct, in fact, that many experts claim that they should always be separated for control purposes. (Liquor is a high-profit operation—and also carries high potential for losses due to free drinks, spillage, pilferage, and simple carelessness.)

If you can isolate costs by operation or product, do so. This is a fringe benefit of preparing for break-even costs. If you can do this, and at the same time allocate the overhead over the same operations or products, you can figure break-even by product line. This can lead to all sorts of surprises —as noted by many manufacturers.

Apply the break-even formula

While there are a number of formulas available for arriving at break-even, only one will be used here. Don't bother to memorize it. Write it down somewhere and refer to it. The actual calculation is purely mechanical.

$$\text{Break-even Sales in \$'s} = \text{Fixed Costs} + 1 - \frac{\text{Variable Costs}}{\text{Sales Volume}}$$

To convert the break-even sales in dollars to units, divide it by the sales price per unit. This is one place where splitting your costs into product lines is handy—not that every business lends itself to such precision, of course. Once again, be reasonable. You may find that expressing break-even in units is more descriptive than expressing it in dollars—and certainly many sales managers prefer such a breakdown because it can be graphically presented to the sales force.

Take total variable costs and divide it by the sales volume associated with those costs. This should result in a fraction less than one. Subtract this fraction from one and the result should be another fraction less than one. Divide your fixed costs by this latter fraction and the result will be your break-even sales volume.

What, in fact, has been done? When total variable costs are divided by the associated sales volume, the resulting fraction put in decimal form is the number of cents of variable cost incurred for every dollar of sales. If total costs are, for example, $3,000, and the associated sales volume is $4,000, the resulting fraction is .75. This means that for every dollar of sales, 75 cents worth of variable costs are

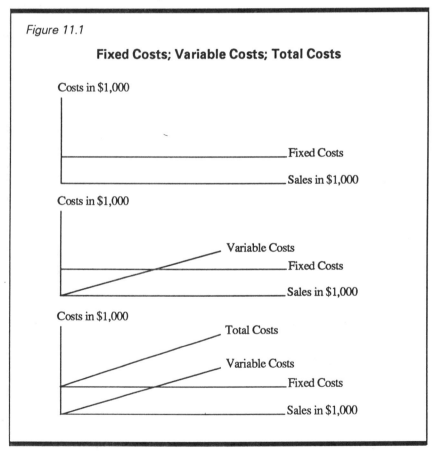

Figure 11.1

Fixed Costs; Variable Costs; Total Costs

incurred. When subtracted from one, the resulting fraction is .25. This means that for every dollar of sales, 25 cents is available to apply to fixed costs. If, in this example, fixed costs total $900, dividing that sum by .25 results in a break-even answer of $3,600. Surprise! The break-even sales volume required is $400 less than the sales volume achieved and the business is profitable. If, in the example, fixed costs were $1,500 instead of $900, dividing .25 into that number results in a break-even volume of $6,000, or $2,000 more than actually achieved.

This analysis helps explain the phenomenon of running harder and harder to stay in the same place—many small businesses can never quite reach break-even because their fixed costs (interest, for example) are too high.

Schematically, you make a graph for break-even as shown in Figure 11.2. Figure 11.1, shows how the fixed cost line together with the variable cost line gives the total cost line.

You can see that the analysis is set forth graphically as in Figure 11.2. As sales rise out to the right, costs rise up the scale. But total costs do not begin at zero as do sales, since there is a fixed costs component of $900 no matter what sales are.

This graphic presentation is most useful for assessing "the trend" at a glance, over time. Monthly sales can be plotted on the total sales line and fairly soon it becomes clear when your business will reach break-even.

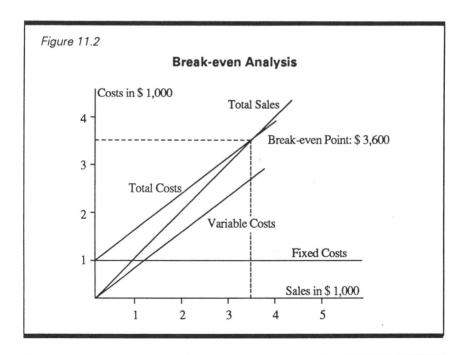

Figure 11.2

Break-even Analysis

Use the break-even insights

Applying the formula gives the basic desired result—you will know what your break-even volume of sales must be, given your current cost conditions or forecasts.

But this is only where the fun begins if you want to make a real working tool of the break-even formula. For example, the 25 cents left over after the variable costs have been taken out of the sales dollar is not only the contribution to fixed costs. That 25 cents represents the amount of profit to be expected out of each sales dollar once break-even volume has been achieved. In the example given, the business owner can expect to receive a profit of 25 cents on each dollar of sales over $3,600. If he forecasts his sales for the period at $9,000, he can expect to earn about $1,350 in profits. If his fixed costs are $1,500 instead of $900, he can see that he will reach break-even at $6,000—and forecast profits of $750.

Applying the formula can be painful. Conventional financial statements vary in their capacity to present operating data in a manner that answers some of the more important questions you may ask.

For example, take the fraction:

$$\frac{\text{Total Variable Cost}}{\text{Sales Volume}}$$

An egg processor in financial difficulties was convinced that an increase in his sales volume from 3 million dozen to 4 million dozen eggs per year would solve his problems. He thought that an increase in volume was the answer. The egg processor, looking at his financial statements, saw that after subtracting cost of goods sold, he had a gross profit margin of about 15%. What he did not realize was that buried down in general expenses were such items as trucking expenses to haul the eggs to market, drivers' wages, fuel oil to heat the chicken coops, and other quite directly variable expenses. When all the variable costs were collected and placed in the fractions, the end result was something like this:

$$\frac{\text{Variable Costs: } \$ 1,050,000}{\text{Sales Volume: } \quad 950,000}$$

$$\frac{\text{Variable Costs:}}{\text{Sales Volume:}} = 1.105$$

For every dollar of sales, he was incurring a direct loss before fixed costs of 10.5 cents. An increase in volume would only drive him deeper into the hole.

Financial statements can lead to false hopes in another manner—which is exposed by the break-even equation. A brick manufacturer looking at his financial statements saw that for the past few years he had been losing about $20,000 per year on sales volume of over two million dollars. He was convinced that such a relatively small loss could be easily overcome by an increased sales effort. But when the variable cost to total sales fraction was computed, the result was .93, meaning that only 7 cents was available to put against fixed costs out of every dollar of sales. At that rate, sales would have to be increased by over $285,000 just to break even, and by over $570,000 to make a profit of $20,000 instead of a loss.

It's nice to have a hefty fraction of each sales dollar to apply to fixed costs and profit—but just how nice it is depends on how high fixed costs are in relation to sales. Many businesses have solid margins but still lose money because fixed costs are too high relative to sales. This kind of problem is often less hopeless than the one where variable costs are greater than sales, but in many instances, fixed costs are far more difficult to pare than variable ones. In the long run, rent has to be paid, the bank has to be satisfied, insurance premiums come due.

The results of break-even analysis can be applied in yet another manner. An importer of clothing was selling both in a retail store and by mail order. The mail order volume was some four or five times larger than that of the retail store, and the owners were convinced that future profits were to be found in mail order.

However, by allocating costs and running a break-even analysis on each portion of the business after the first year, the owners made a startling discovery: the ratio of retail sales to retail break-even was .98. In other words, the retail operation was 98% of the way towards breaking even in the first year. But the ratio of mail order sales to mail order break-even was only .53—that is, only 53% of the way towards breaking even. These results caused some major reallocation of effort.

So far, the major emphasis has been on the sales volume required to break even at a stated combination of fixed and variable costs. The same break-even techniques can also be extremely useful in answering "what if?" questions regarding cost reductions for a given level of sales.

A reduction of one dollar in fixed costs has far more impact than a reduction of one dollar in variable costs.

Why? Take the example where:

Sales volume   = $ 4,000
Variable costs = $ 3,000
Fixed costs   = $ 900

Break-even volume was $3,600, and for each dollar of sales, 25 cents was available to apply towards fixed costs and profits. If variable costs for the same period are reduced by $100, the equation is as follows:

Break-even= $\dfrac{\$\ 900}{1-\dfrac{2,900}{4,000}}$ or $ 3,272

However, if fixed costs are reduced $100 for the same period, the break-even equation is:

Break-even= $\dfrac{\$\ 800}{1-\dfrac{3,000}{4,000}}$ or $ 3,200

Why does the break-even point change so much more if fixed costs are reduced than if variable costs are reduced? Reducing variable costs in our example by $100 only increases the amount of each sales dollar left over to apply to fixed costs and profits by 2.5 cents. Reducing the fixed costs by $100 freed up 25 cents of every sales dollar for every dollar of fixed cost reduction.

When budgeting or forecasting, break-even analysis is a simple and quick device for testing alternative strategies. Advertising expenditures are a good case in point. Advertising can be treated as either a variable or a fixed cost, depending on the strategy adopted by the business owner. If he or she decides that advertising expenditures for the coming year are going to be $5,000 no matter what the level of sales, then they are fixed. On the other hand, if $100 will be spent each month for every $10,000 in sales the preceding month, then advertising costs will be variable.

While it may be difficult to estimate the impact on sales of a proposed advertising campaign, by using break-even analysis you can estimate what additional increase in sales must result from an increase in expenditures in order to justify the additional advertising costs.

Take our example again. If the owner wants to test the needed sales increase to justify an additional $100 advertising expense, fixed costs become $1,000.

Plugging the numbers into the formula gives a new break-even figure of $4,000. Since break-even had been $3,600, at least $400 in additional sales must be generated just to remain even.

Please note that other considerations enter the advertising decision. The break-even approach is just a tool, not a decision-making machine.

This all comes back to a point made earlier: deciding whether a cost is fixed or variable obviously makes a difference. Yet many years of experience in applying break-even analysis leads to the conclusion that the recommendation made earlier in this topic is still the best. Either quickly and arbitrarily assign a given cost to one or the other category, or add up all of these semi-variable costs and assign half to each category.

And in the long run, be aware of one important point. Fixed costs do not remain fixed forever, or through the entire range of possible sales volumes. When sales get large enough, more space is needed and rent will go up. When deliveries become more numerous, new trucks may be needed and their cost, too, will rise.

Conversely, if sales fall off enough, one secretary will suffice where two had been needed, office salaries will fall, fixed assets may be sold to retire debt. And so forth—these are not permanently fixed.

Most simply put, break-even analysis is a powerful tool for analyzing your business and helping you make the right decisions for your business. But like all tools, it is only effective if used carefully by the right person in the right areas.

By relating fixed and variable costs to sales levels, break-even analysis also will help you to focus on the aspects of your company that you can affect—and help you to accept the costs you have little or no control over. By putting these items in perspective, you can more easily avoid rash decisions, identify the more sensible strategies for your business to follow, and do a better job of managing your business.

How to categorize costs

The following extended example of cost assignment is based on a real restaurant consulting job.

The consultant used a quick and arbitrary approach to assigning these semi-variable costs to their fixed or variable category rather than the other recommended method of adding them up, dividing the total by two, and thus making the assignment.

Food cost: Variable.

Beverage cost: Variable.

Salaries and wages: Not including the owner's draw. Variable. While there is some fixed component to this because someone must be on hand while the restaurant is open even if no customers show up, most of the help is on a part-time basis, so that wages are geared fairly directly to the volume of business.

Payroll taxes: Variable. These are tied to salaries and wages.

Rent: Fixed for any reasonable accounting period.

Advertising: Variable. For the owner the relationship is inverse: when sales are down, advertising is increased; when sales are up, he tapers off on this cost.

Utilities: Fixed. Unless there were to be a drastic shift in the hours this restaurant is open, occasioned, perhaps, by a dramatic change in sales volume, the basic utilities are independent of volume. Ovens, for instance, must be hot—and the building must be heated or cooled whether there are two or two hundred customers.

Depreciation: Fixed. This can change if assets are added or disposed of.

Interest: Fixed.

Repairs and maintenance: Fixed, though in many operations of this sort considered variable.

Liquor license: Fixed.

Rubbish removal: In this case, fixed. Pick-up is twice a week on a contractual basis—in many other restaurants, where disposal is on a per can fee, this is variable.

Travel: Fixed. In fact, the year-end operating results dictate whether the owner goes to a plush hospitality trade convention; for the past ten years he has gone.

China and glassware: Variable. The breakage is directly related to sales levels.

Group insurance: Variable. Tied to wages and salaries.

Contributions: Fixed. But you can bet that they will go down next year if this year is a poor one.

Vehicle expense: Fixed. This restaurant does not deliver, and the car is a fringe benefit for the owner.

Insurance: Fixed. In many cases, certain premiums are tied to the volume of sales and would be a variable cost.

Consulting fees: Fixed.

Legal and accounting: Fixed. If someone were to sue, this could rise—but it is independent of volume.

Telephone: Fixed. For a different operation, this could be variable.

Music and entertainment: Fixed. No matter how many people are in the place, the owner provides entertainment two nights a week.

Action Plan For:
"Break-even Analysis"

❏ Determine which costs are fixed and which are variable at a given time and under a reasonably constant set of circumstances.

❏ Figure out how to allocate semi-variable costs.

❏ Calculate the break-even volume by dividing fixed costs by one minus variable costs divided by sales volume.

❏ Plot your monthly figures on a graph so you can assess the trend over time.

❏ Put the insights you gain into action: for example, pare fixed costs if necessary, give the most profitable aspects of your business the attention they deserve, and test alternative strategies when you're forecasting or budgeting before you take action.

Chapter Twelve:

Pricing Strategies

....

Once you know what sales are needed for your company to break even, you'll be ready to focus on establishing pricing objectives. Pricing requires a delicate sense of balance. Prices not only have to make a profit, they have to lure in customers. Your prices must be competitive or your customers will desert you, unless you can offer attractive non-price factors such as convenient hours, personal service, or a reputation for quality and reliability. Your prices must be high enough to cover all your operating and selling expenses. These include your overhead costs—such as rent, insurance, interest payments—as well as your variable costs, such as direct sales expense, sales commissions, inventory carrying costs, and so on. Most importantly, your prices must produce a reasonable profit. Don't undersell yourself or the commodities you have to offer—pay yourself well for the time you spend.

As you consider your pricing objectives, shape them into a definite quantity whenever possible. "More profit" is not a definite quantity. "Increase gross margin from 38.6 percent to 40.4 percent" is. Once your objectives are clear, you can work on reaching them.

Devising a pricing strategy is (as you know) a complex matter which demands attention to detail and careful thought. Numerous factors affect your prices—from inventory carrying costs to purchasing methods to location. And once you've come up with a reasonable pricing strategy, you've got to make it work—and continue to make it work. The steps outlined in this chapter will make that task easier.

The four approaches to pricing

How do you establish the right price for your goods and services? Chances are you follow at least one of the four pricing approaches:

1. Full-cost pricing
2. Flexible markups
3. Gross margin
4. Suggested or going rate

Of these four pricing methods, the most widely used is full-cost pricing, also called cost plus or percent over cost. The most realistic method of pricing, though, contains elements of all four.

The intent of this chapter is to help you to identify a range of prices for your products which ties in with your marketing plans, your cost structure, your production/distribution constraints, and your competitive position. The six steps of establishing prices are the same for all businesses. There are substantial differences, of course, between the concerns a manufacturer faces and those a wholesale distributor might face—but the concepts are the same.

Ultimately, your pricing structure must meet a number of apparently conflicting concerns. They must cover your direct or variable costs. For example, the material and labor involved in producing a product, and the packaging, shipping, and freight costs tied directly to volume of sales must be covered. Overhead (or fixed) costs such as rent, insurance, interest payments, and so forth must also be covered. If both direct and overhead costs are not covered, then your pricing structure guarantees problems.

In many businesses, lack of attention to important cost areas can lead to selling goods or services at a loss. If you are losing $1 on each unit sale, then increased sales will only put you deeper into debt—a problem which is far more common than many people realize. Your pricing must provide profit. Sooner or later your business stands or falls on its ability to generate consistent operating profits. If revenues do not exceed costs, it is extremely difficult to justify continuing a business.

The classic dilemma is whether to choose high volume and low prices or high prices and low volume. Low prices tend to increase market share at the expense of profits, while high prices tend to lower market share and risk pricing the product or service out of the market entirely. Balancing these conflicts requires careful attention to costs, marketing objectives, price sensitivity in the market, and a host of other factors. As you move from pricing objectives to actual pricing strategy, you will ordinarily have established a range of possible prices in which the lowest price represents the minimum amount necessary to cover your costs, and the top price represents the perceived value to the buyer.

The perceived value to the buyer is an important pricing concept. The price you place on a product includes quality, distribution, credit, warranties, and a number of less-than-obvious factors which add to or subtract from the value of your product or service as seen by the market.

Perceived value is directly linked to the image a company projects. This is especially important to information or service-oriented companies that have "intangibles" to sell. Consider the plight of an advertising agency. The agency must convince clients they have the specialized expertise and information necessary to create a successful sales and product image. The client must recognize that an intangible such as a logo design is actually worth a sizable fee, that image and advertising are crucial to sales. A courageous hourly rate, rather than deterring potential customers, may create an image of professional quality and expertise.

Price =
Image + Service + Product

Here's an example of this formula: You can purchase a bicycle in a number of different ways. You can go to the discount store and buy a disassembled bicycle in a carton. You would not know whether the bicycle was the right one for your purposes, you would not know whether spare parts would be available if needed, and you would have the headache of going home and assembling the bicycle yourself with no aid beyond whatever tools you have at home, your own ingenuity, and an incomplete set of instructions. (We know one doubtful mechanic who bought and tried to assemble such an item. Eventually and sheepishly, he took it to a full-service bike shop and paid them to disentangle his efforts.) With this method of purchase, you may be dealing with a product that is inferior or substandard, non-existent service, and an image that conveys no status.

For a slightly higher price, you could go to your local hardware store or department store and purchase a name-brand bicycle fully assembled, perhaps with a warranty that guarantees moving parts for a year. You would be spared the effort of assembling the bicycle yourself, and you would have the security of knowing that if you lost a part you could get a replacement. Here the product and image are perhaps of better quality, although the service may still be inadequate.

Yet another possibility would be going to a specialty bicycle store. At such a store you would receive expert advice on the best bicycle for your particular needs, how to maintain the bicycle in the best possible condition, perhaps a trade-in on your old bicycle, and some indication of trade-in value if your needs change. A full-service department with trained mechanics would alleviate worries about future maintenance. Further, you might be given information about bicycle clubs, scenic trips in your area, and a variety of highly specialized, individual attention. These extra services and the specialty image would justify higher prices.

It is entirely possible that you could buy the same bicycle at these three places for three radically different prices and yet be satisfied with each. The value you perceive includes the intangibles of service and specialized expertise.

The nature of the product can be the same. If there are substitute products, or different brands, then the comparisons tend to become blurred. But in comparing products or services to their equivalent products or services, some rules will serve to guide your pricing strategies: 1) high margins and high differentiation of products go together; 2) low margins and products with little or no product differentiation go together. For example, there is considerable product differentiation between luxury automobiles, such as Mercedes or Cadillacs, and accordingly, margins are wide. There is almost no differentiation between packages of corn flakes. Not surprisingly, undifferentiated products such as corn flakes tend to have small markups, since there is little to help you choose between one corn flake and another.

A clever manufacturer may justify higher prices by orchestrating a quality image using advertising and packaging. For instance, name-brand items often have snob appeal, while "no-name" goods appeal to the person who compares prices.

Consider the price elasticity of your industry. If a small price rise leads to a large drop in unit sales, the price is said to be elastic. If a big price rise leads to a small drop in unit sales, then the price is said to be inelastic. Industry associations frequently conduct studies of price elasticity, since the information is obviously very important to anyone contemplating changes in their pricing strategy. If your industry conducts such studies, take advantage of it. If you do not have an industry association or if your association does not conduct price elasticity tests, then you may wish to sample small segments of your market.

You can do this informally by asking your customers questions like, "If we increase the price, will you still buy?" Ask your customers to fill out a response card. Give them a small premium for their time. This will give you an idea of how customers perceive your products.

Formally, you can get expert advice or help in sampling market share from most business schools. Or, your trade association will likely have information on how to conduct a market sample. (To locate the appropriate association, see *The Encyclopedia of Associations* published by Gale Research Company, Book Tower, Detroit, Michigan 48226.)

Conducting a market sample can be costly but far less expensive in the long run than suddenly discovering that your sales have evaporated and that you have priced yourself completely out of your market (or less drastically, that you are the last to raise your prices, and your sacrificial price policy did not gain you any market share).

If you ignore price elasticity you risk pricing yourself out of the market. You may get a good customer and believe you've got that customer hooked on your services. Greed takes over. Prices are increased; the customer is lost. Stick to a consistent marketing and pricing strategy and let customers know in advance about legitimate price increases.

All pricing strategies end up as competitive pricing strategies. Your aim should be to at least maintain market share and at the same time improve profits.

How do you meet all these various concerns? By following the step-by-step process detailed below.

Identify pricing objectives

The overall objectives of your business have a direct effect on your pricing objectives.

The most direct route to a realistic pricing policy is to set measurable sales objectives for a clearly defined time span. It doesn't much matter whether you express sales in units or gross dollars, but it does matter that the goals be set in terms of so many units or so many dollars in sales per month. In many cases, sales goals should be tied down even more closely. For seasonal businesses such as those which specialize in brief selling periods (some specialty stores, seasonal hospitality businesses, many agricultural or agriculture-related businesses), it may be important to establish daily sales goals. Your experience is the best guide to your own needs—in your business planning efforts these goals will ordinarily be stated fairly broadly.

The most common objectives are stated in terms of dollar sales, unit sales, and profit. They should be broken down by product line or, if possible, by product.

One small business sold a nutritive doughnut made of wheat germ, whole wheat, and honey which did not absorb grease when deep fried. It was cheap and simple to make, with high profit margins. They received excellent advice from their local business school on how to conduct a market sample. Every customer got a free box of doughnuts for filling out a simple form. Their questions were basic: Why did you buy this product? For its nutritive value? For the packaging? What size package do you prefer? When do you do your shopping?

The results? They discovered that people would pay a high premium for a natural product. They were more apt to buy a medium-sized package (the small packages disappeared too fast, the large ones went stale). Because it was a natural product with no preservatives, it was necessary to know when people did their shopping in order to deal with the constraints of shelf life.

The total profit you gain from a product comes by multiplying the number of units sold times the dollar contribution per unit. Dollar contribution per unit may be difficult to establish on a product basis since it involves detailed cost and price information. In the simplest case, you would figure the dollar contribution by unit by subtracting the costs associated with the sale of that unit (including a share of the overhead costs) from the price you sell the unit for. Since this information is extremely difficult to generate for most businesses, a more common practice is to concentrate on sales volume, which allows you to aggregate all the expenses and work directly from your income statement projection. Sales volume is calculated by multiplying the number of units sold by the price. The problem with working on sales volume as opposed to total profit is that it is very possible for parts of your product line to be losing money while other parts are your breadwinners.

To their chagrin, restaurateurs sometimes find they lose money on their food while they derive profit from liquor sales. A full-service department in a retail store may not be profitable in itself, but that may be outweighed by the sales advantages of convenient in-house repair.

The objectives of increasing sales volume, moreover, may frequently come in conflict with the objectives of increasing profits. For marketing reasons, it may be far more important to sacrifice short-term profits for long-term increase in market share, or to establish your business in new markets, or to introduce new products. Increased sales volume does not always lead to increased profits.

The difficulty of setting objectives can easily be overrated. Most business owners balance these concerns handily—but if you are aware of how they interact and how profits and sales volume can affect each other in your business, then you will be far ahead of your competitors.

Establish price ranges

There is no mechanical method of establishing the ideal pricing for your products or services. There are too many outside forces which will affect the "ideal price," and there is some question as to whether such an ideal price can be defined at all. The common sense approach to pricing requires that you establish price ranges on a product or service basis.

The bottom of the price range can be established by performing a simple break-even analysis. Break-even represents the sales level at which your business neither makes a profit nor experiences a loss. Determining the break-even sales volume can be difficult, particularly if you have products selling at different prices with a number of variable costs which fluctuate.

Another approach is to estimate the number of units to be sold, then experiment with different prices to see how many units at different prices are needed to cover your fixed expenses. An important part of this calculation involves inventory turn: How many times does your average inventory fit into your annual cost of goods sold? If your average inventory is $50,000 and your annual cost of goods sold is $300,000, then you would be said to have turned your inventory six times. Knowing how many times you turn your inventory is particularly helpful if you have a lot of products which move at different speeds. Once again, you can get bogged down in detail if you try to figure price range on an item-by-item basis.

At the other end of the scale is the nebulous figure often described as "what the market will bear." Your customers will pay no more for your goods or services than they have to. Their perception of the value of your product or service establishes a very effective upper price limit.

This is one of the areas where your long-term objectives must be seriously considered. It may be possible to charge a very high price for goods or products to attain high short-term profits—for example, think about the practice of scalping tickets to the Super Bowl. With a product in very short supply, with a very high perceived value, a scalper can make a substantial profit—but if the scalper wishes to maintain a long-term relationship with the clients, that is, plans to become a legitimate ticket agency, the pricing strategy will have to change.

How can you determine the upper range? You can experiment.

It is far more common to underprice goods and services than to overprice them; for example, one company we know was charging major corporate customers $750 a year for a service that 12 months later was being marketed just as easily for $6000 to the same clients. Even if it were eight times more difficult to sell the service, for $6000 the profits would have been the same or greater at the higher price. The cost of servicing one major client is far less than catering to many small customers.

The purpose of establishing a price range is to enable you to move away from irrational pricing forced upon you by your competitors. Base price ranges on your perception of the value of what you sell, your need to maintain operating profitability, and business objectives. Such a policy can be far more in your control than you might expect.

Define competitive pricing strategy

It's time to return to the four most common approaches to pricing, which are all designed to put you in an advantageous competitive position. The commonsensible pricing approach uses elements of all four methods. If you understand all of them, you can pick and choose the best method for your business at any given time.

1. Full-Cost Pricing

If you can identify all of your operating costs, all you need to do is distribute these costs to the merchandise costs, add a preset figure for profit, and grind out the prices. If all costs are taken into consideration and a profit is added, then assuming that you meet your sales objectives, you have to make money.

There are two weaknesses in this method. The merchandise must be sold, and it must be sold in sufficient quantity to push you past the break-even point. A rigid pricing policy such as full-cost suffers from the same problem inherent in any rigid approach: It ignores the effects of a changing, fickle marketplace.

The great advantage of full-cost pricing is that it simplifies the pricing decision. You or your accountant generate the cost figures and decide how much profit you wish to make (presumably this profit level is realistic—we assume that the profit objective is not based on wishful thinking).

Many businesses claim to figure their prices on a full-cost basis. Very few actually do. However, it does provide a guideline, and many business owners use the full-cost approach as another method of establishing or narrowing price ranges.

2. Flexible Markups

The flexible markup system is less rigid than the full-cost approach and is particularly useful during periods of rapidly changing prices. To use the flexible approach, you must determine whether your goods or services are price sensitive. If the pricing is inelastic, then be courageous in your pricing. If your market is sensitive to price changes, then you must be far more cautious. Unlike the fixed price approach, the flexible approach allows you to experiment with a variety of marketing techniques, such as loss leaders (where you sell certain goods or services at reduced prices in order to get the customer to buy other products or services), different price structures for different product lines to provide a wider range of options for your customer, or using prices to differentiate similar products. It is by no means uncommon for manufacturers to market identical products to different markets at radically different prices. The full-cost approach to pricing tends to rule out this kind of marketing.

Remember that your aim is to generate operating profits. However, if you are selling a product which suddenly becomes obsolete, you might wish to sell it at a severe loss to get it off the books and off your inventory. (Remember the hula hoop?)

A trendy or short-lived product or service in high demand must be handled carefully. Take advantage of a trend in its early and lucrative stages. A large stock of technologically outdated or novelty merchandise that won't move, no matter how much you lower your prices, can be crippling to a business. One entrepreneur, during the roller skate craze, bought out an entire factory of metal-wheeled skates, only to have fantasies of future fortune smashed by the advent of plastic wheels. Again, a flexible pricing approach allows you to rapidly unload a product.

The danger of the flexible approach is that in pursuit of sales, profits may be lost or given away. Tension often arises between production and sales personnel over this flexible pricing approach. Salespeople want to promise or give away anything in order to lure in more customers, while production insists on higher rates, wishing to avoid servicing unprofitable accounts or living up to unrealistic promises of overeager sales reps. The full-cost approach prevents falling below an acceptable range of profitability (assuming that the product can be sold). The flexible approach is frequently abused, and in order to maintain daily sales quotas, loss leaders are sold by the bushel while the profit-makers remain on the shelves.

3. Gross Margin

Gross margin pricing can be calculated in two ways. For markup, calculate a percentage of your wholesale cost and add it back to the wholesale cost to establish the sales cost. Mark-on refers to a percent of the retail price that the gross margin represents.

The gross margin approach takes operating costs and market factors into account. As with the full-cost approach, the intention of the price strategy will be achieved only if sufficient sales volume is generated. Ordinarily, different margins will be applied to different products. This gives more flexibility than is possible under a full-cost approach. If you know which items are price sensitive and which are not, and if you can vary the markup accordingly, your profits will benefit. You want to establish a regular markup as a guide to pricing decisions, but not use it as a rigid method—because the rigid methods tend to lock you into price structures which may not be realistic over the long haul.

If you have a hammer that costs you $4.85 and apply 60 percent markup, the retail price of that hammer would be $7.76. This price also represents a gross margin contribution or a mark-on of 37.5 percent.

Many managers use gross margin pricing to establish a price floor. If you historically need a gross margin of 37.5 percent (for example), that $7.76 figure will probably not be adequate. However, it will prevent gross underpricing and will afford a starting point for a further series of questions. For each item ask yourself whether it will move swiftly or slowly, whether there is a risk that it will not sell at all, and what the top price would be for your market for that item. Every business has a different set of questions appropriate to its product or service line. Depending on the result of your analysis, the final price you put on the product should be moved up or, in rare cases, down from the floor established by gross margin pricing.

Figure 12.1

Price Range Guidelines

Item _____

Price Ranges $ _____ to $ _____ .

1. Price Floor
   - Mark-on (gross margin) is ____% of retail price.
   - Manufacturer's suggested price is _____.
   - Fixed costs are _____. Variable costs are _____.
   - Break-even point is _____.

2. Special consideration for this product's or service's price are:
   - ☐ service
   - ☐ status
   - ☐ superior quality
   - ☐ use as a loss leader
   - ☐ demand/product life
   - ☐ overhead
   - ☐ down time
   - ☐ competitive position
   - ☐ market penetration costs

3. Turnover rate is _____ times per year.

4. Industry average is _____.

5. Going rate is _____.

6. I estimate _____ units will be sold.

7. Top price possible is _____. (Estimate customer's perception of value.)

Comments: _____

_____

---

4. Suggested or Going Rate

Suggested or going rate pricing is the simplest pricing method going. It is also the least satisfactory, since it ignores your own cost structure. If your business has a cost structure that approximates industry averages, then suggested or going rate pricing will provide only mediocre profits—assuming that the industry itself is profitable.

Once you know your industry's traditional markup patterns, you must determine whether or not you can afford to be in business within these established margins. Before following going rate pricing, first determine whether sales will be sufficient at that price to cover all selling and operating expenses and provide a reasonable profit.

This kind of pricing method places you in a catch-up position: You have to look and see what other people are doing before establishing your prices, then you set your prices, but always after the competition has set theirs.

Following the lead of the competition does save you some paperwork, but we suggest you use this method only as an adjunct to other methods. If your prices are way out of line with those of the competition, it is to your advantage to be aware of the variances and the reasons for them. Many businesses follow manufacturers' suggested pricing or play follow the leader and spend most of their time observing each other before taking any action at all. Being a leader may pay you rich dividends. As a follower, average profits will be the best you can do.

The competitive pricing strategy that will pay off the most in the long run is one which takes advantage of the strengths of all four possible pricing approaches. By using full-cost and gross margin pricing methods to establish the lowest price you can afford, while maintaining the flexibility of a flexible markup system, you will avoid being trapped in a rigid, mechanical price structure. If you keep your eye on the competition and on manufacturers' suggested prices, where pertinent, and in all cases keep your own cost structure in mind, you should be able to establish optimum price ranges for your products.

Consider the impact of product lines, inventory, and selling costs on pricing

Some of the more important things you have to keep in mind in establishing prices are:

1. Product lines

You may find it necessary to sell some items at or below cost in order to fill out a product line. This obviously depends on the kind of business you are in; it may be more expensive in the long run to stock and sell only those items on which you make a profit than to stock and sell some items below cost in order to entice customers to purchase other items from you. Any full service department in a retail store must carry, or have ready access to, parts needed to service the line carried in that store, regardless of the profitability of carrying some items.

2. Current carrying costs of inventory (including financing, storage, shipping, and handling costs)

Find out what the current carrying cost for inventory is and ask your accountant for help in factoring this cost into your pricing structure. If you have to maintain a large inventory that turns very slowly, this factor will be more important than if you have a small inventory which you turn frequently. For most businesses involved in purchasing items for resale, the cost of carrying inventory has risen sharply over the past few years and has had a severe effect on bottom line profits.

Beware of bargains from wholesalers. Discount prices at this level generally indicate the merchandise in question is slow moving or about to be superseded by a new or improved line. A large quantity of outdated stock on your shelves for years to come is no bargain. Slow-moving merchandise costs money. Imprudent purchases may ultimately force you to sell the items at a loss simply to regain some capital. (Remember that sales should be short and attractive—a real contrast to normal prices.) It is sometimes preferable to stay with established merchandise at the going rate and realize a turnover at a smaller margin. With your recouped cash, you can purchase something with a more rapid turnover and greater volume of sales, and thus generate more profit.

It's important to keep systematized control of your inventory in order to keep your costs from skyrocketing. Careful inventory control helps eliminate pilferage and costly duplication. One full-service department, while attempting to organize inventory, discovered five separate cases of parts duplication. With no inventory system, items were lost or forgotten and reordered, a waste of time and money. It was also discovered that many items that had previously been ordered in bulk at the beginning of the season (many had become obsolete) could be ordered a few at a time, as needed, without tying up limited space and capital. Occasionally you want to buy specific items in economical quantities, but they should be real movers or be used as loss leaders to entice more customers.

3. Other costs associated with pricing

It is not enough just to establish the more obvious costs associated with pricing. Many businesses, especially newer businesses or those businesses with high, variable selling costs, find that a sizable portion of the pricing decision rests on establishing the selling costs of each item. For example, if your accounting system does not help you break out the selling costs associated with each product or service that you sell, you may be inadvertently giving away the store. If you can ascertain your selling costs on a product or service line basis, you may find that some products or services are far more profitable than others—and that the profit-makers are not the ones you would have picked as your breadwinners. Some large accounts take up so much selling and servicing time that they actually detract from your profits.

Choose a flexible pricing approach

Be sure to examine your pricing alternatives. Since the price represents the sum of the product plus service plus an image factor, you have a wide range of alternatives to consider. The most common competitive approach is to try to gain market share by cutting prices. For instance, an ad agency competing for smaller ad dollars by slashing prices found, to their dismay, that those losses could not be afforded. "Most common" does not translate to "most sensible" for many businesses. There are alternatives to price competition; these include service, location, customization, expertise, image, follow-through, stability, predictability, geniality, and many other possibilities. Name your own.

Suppose you discover your sales are down and those proceeds will soon be insufficient to cover your operating and selling expenses. Your immediate reaction might be to increase your prices. An alternative to that pricing approach (which may lose you customers and cause your sales volume to plummet) might be to attempt to increase the volume of sales. You need to determine your price-vol-

---

Figure 12.2

Setting Prices

Consider setting prices just *above* your competitors' prices if:	Consider setting prices just *below* your competitors' prices if:
• Your market is inelastic.	• Your market is highly elastic.
• Your market consists mainly of growing commercial customers.	• You're attempting to enter a new market.
• Your product is an integral part of an established system.	• Your customers need to reorder parts or supplies.
• Your reputation for status, service, etc., increases your product's perceived value.	• Your business is small enough that a lower price won't threaten your larger competitors.
• Your customers can easily build your price into their selling price.	• You have the option of economical production runs which decrease your unit cost.
• Your product is only a tiny percentage of your customers' total costs.	• You have not reached full production capacity.

---

ume-profit relationship. By comparing selling price with the number of items sold, you can discover which price would raise the most revenue. Remember that your image of being fair-priced and offering good value is something you don't want to jeopardize with arbitrary price hikes. Higher markups might just make things worse. Increasing volume may be the answer to increased expenses. In that case, you must work on your image, sales, and distribution methods to generate those increased sales.

Markdowns and loss leaders can also be used to increase sales, but should be used carefully. Always keep in mind that your overall sales must cover your costs and leave you a profit. Markdowns should be used with dead or slow-moving stock, or items priced too high to begin with. Consider a markdown when you have sudden competition on an item. Also, with careful monitoring of your accounting and inventory systems, you may find you have reached your projected sales level and can afford to lower your markup to entice new customers.

Psychology is another factor to consider when determining prices. We are all aware that selling an item for "only $19.99" has a greater consumer appeal than the same item at $20. The dollar figure registers first, and the customer subconsciously thinks the price is less.

Status and prestige are other psychological factors to consider in your pricing strategy. Remember that there is an element of prestige involved in the price of an item. An exceptional bargain on an expensive item may spur the customer to look for flaws. One midwestern manufacturer of a high-quality speaker marketed at low cost was amazed that sales were so poor. After consulting a marketing specialist, he raised his prices from $400 to $850. At the lower price, customers would not believe the speaker was of good quality, whereas the higher price bespoke both quality and prestige.

High prices sometimes encourage, rather than inhibit, sales (Rolls Royces, mink coats, caviar). Sport shoe manufacturers, for instance, constantly vie for the "classy" image and the corresponding price.

The four pricing approaches discussed in this chapter help narrow the ranges of pricing alternatives. Once you have narrowed the range and have decided which questions to ask yourself and how to reach pricing decisions, you would be smart to make that pricing approach policy for your business. Write it down. You can always change the approach if it does not work, but unless you know how you arrive at your prices—what rationale lies behind your pricing decisions—you will find it very difficult to arrive at the best pricing structure for your business.

We keep referring to a flexible pricing approach. Pricing is an art. There is no simple, mechanical method of calculating prices. You have to be sensitive to your competitors' prices, shifts in population, fluctuations in interest rates, the amount of your market's discretionary income, and other outside forces that affect the perceived value of what you sell. It may be more profitable to dump inventory at what appears to be a loss than to hold on to it hoping for an upturn in the economy. Consider once more the Super Bowl ticket scalper. What is the value of a Super Bowl ticket the day after the game?

Flexible does not mean wishy-washy, vacillating, hit or miss, or whimsical. Choosing a flexible pricing approach means that you must be aware of the factors affecting the prices of your goods or services on an ongoing basis and be able ideally to foresee opportunities to change your prices to gain maximum advantage. That is why rigid full-cost or gross margin pricing is not recommended. You have to be flexible to take advantage of opportunities. By the time the industry averages reflect ephemeral changes, those changes have gone. Others will have gained the benefits; the business locked into a rigid price structure will miss them.

As an analogy, a broken watch is accurate twice a day. The same is true of a rigid pricing schedule structure—it may be right on target when the market is going up and right on target when the market goes down, but between those points lies a lot of lost profit.

Implement and monitor pricing strategy

Your long-range goals are achieved by consistent use of a series of interlocking short-term strategies. By establishing a flexible pricing approach, one which helps you avoid underpricing by using the best aspects of full-cost or gross margin pricing corrected by experience and current market conditions, you should end up with a workable strategy that is consistent and understandable.

Keep in mind that no one approach, no matter how carefully thought out, will always yield the best pricing strategy. Once you have chosen your pricing approach, you must implement it. Once you have implemented it, you must monitor that pricing strategy in order to make sure that it is still adequate. If you find that your market share is going down due to poor pricing or that your profits are going down, you have to be ready to react swiftly.

Ordinarily, you would wish to anticipate pricing difficulties. There will be times when you can't—but if you do not carefully and consistently monitor the effectiveness of your pricing strategy, you can be assured that you will build in some pricing errors.

Any planning effort, pricing included, must be reviewed systematically, thoroughly, and frequently. Depending on your business, you will wish to review your pricing strategy at least quarterly, perhaps more frequently.

Your prices have to produce profits. That doesn't mean unfair or unreasonable prices, but it does mean that your prices have an enormous impact on the success of your business.

Action Plan For:
"Pricing Strategies"

❏ Determine the pricing objectives of your business by setting measurable sales objectives for a defined time span.

❏ Establish your price ranges by using break-even analysis to determine your bottom line.

❏ Choose your competitive pricing strategy from the four approaches to pricing.

❏ Consider the impact of the following on your pricing strategy: product lines, current carrying cost of inventory, the selling costs of each product or service.

❏ Maintain a flexible approach in your pricing so you can make the most of opportunities and be sensitive to market changes.

❏ Monitor your pricing strategy and make changes when they're called for.

Chapter Thirteen:

An Approach to Problem Solving

....

Part One: What's the problem?

Now that you've covered the basics for "selling smarter," your next task is to continue building upon your successes. But as you do, you'll inevitably encounter situations you may not have anticipated. Whatever they are, they needn't become problems if you know how to find solutions.

Problem solving is a skill every owner/manager needs, yet it is seldom treated as a skill we can improve upon. While there is no simple method that always leads to correct problem solving and/or decision making, there are tried and true processes to improve the quality of managerial problem solving. This chapter presents a workable approach.

Problem solving begins with the recognition and identification of a problem. If you can recognize when you have a problem, identify the limits of the problem, and can determine more or less what to do about it, you are well on the way to becoming a better problem solver.

Problem solving falls into two parts. The first three steps help to identify and define a problem; the remaining steps are a sketch of how to seek out, evaluate, and choose a rational solution to the problem defined by the first three steps.

Problem recognition: deviation from a standard

All problems share one characteristic: They represent some deviation or variance from a standard. You cannot have a problem unless you have a standard from which to measure deviation.

For example, a sales increase of 15 percent could represent a significant shortfall if the standard called for a sales increase of 30 percent. On the other hand, if the sales increase had been targeted at 5 percent, a 15 percent increase is still a problem, though with different effects.

In both instances the sign of a problem is the deviation from the standard of a budgeted sales increase. Standards needn't be numerical, however. Take quality standards, for example. In the case of a printer, print quality must be equal to a certain standard. A print run deviating from this standard indicates the presence of a problem even if no numbers are involved. Another non-numerical area with explicit standards is personnel management. Job descriptions, personnel manuals, and performance reviews make work standards explicit, which in turn makes spotting personnel problems far simpler than they might be otherwise.

Where do you establish standards? Usually in your business plan—financial projections, product or service descriptions, output schedules, and the like should provide you with detailed sets of standards by which to measure your company's progress.

If you do not have such standards, then recognizing problems as they occur becomes tricky. You will be able to say that something is wrong, but that is a far cry from recognizing what the specific problem is.

The first step in solving a problem presupposes that you have determined which objectives or measurable standards you can measure your progress against. Periodically, compare actual performance against budgeted or projected performance. Deviation analysis can help pinpoint problems, and often does so before a problem becomes too severe. For more obvious problems, knowing the applicable standards helps to determine the severity and importance of a problem, and allows you to manage more rationally. If you can solve the most important problems and distinguish these from less important concerns, your time will be more productively spent.

Deviation analysis attempts to organize business information so you can spot problems before they get out of hand. Two critical controls, cash flow projections (or budget) and the income statement, are extremely sensitive indicators of underlying problems. Please note that a deviation in a particular category may or may not directly point to an underlying problem. Some practice applying deviation analysis will help you to determine when you have a problem which indeed needs action, and when you have a problem which is a momentary wrinkle in your operation, one which is caused by the accounting cycle. (Suppose you paid two monthly utility bills in January, none in February. This will warp your figures on a monthly basis—but not on a year-to-date basis.)

If you do not have a standard against which to measure your progress, yet you feel you can still recognize problems, you are most likely using an internal set of measurements as a standard. This is a risky approach, since it's easy to bend standards to fit realities. Careful use of problem analysis is your best bet—an analysis based on carefully stated (written) standards.

Problem analysis: define the problem, its limits and boundaries

Suppose a product which you manufacture comes off the assembly line in a mangled form. The standard of a quality product has been violated. Or suppose one of your clerks explodes at a customer. An implicit and important standard of courtesy has been violated.

In any case, you know that a problem has popped up. Now your job is to define the problem, to determine its limits, its boundaries, its location, and/or extent. Here, once again, the necessity of measurable or determinable standards is important. It doesn't do much good, for example, to say, "Sales are way out of whack" or "The help is grumpy." It may be true that sales are out of line or that personnel are disagreeable, but until you can decide what the sales are as compared with what they are not, or who is disagreeable (and why), it will be difficult to arrive at an adequate solution to the problem. Such pertinent questions as "Are all products selling slowly or just some?" "Is it a problem this month or has it been a problem for the past several months?" must be answered.

A problem well defined is almost solved. As you define a problem, one possible solution often becomes preeminent. However: Do not jump to a conclusion. Much time is wasted applying hasty conclusions that would be better spent in carefully defining problems. A Problem Analysis Worksheet, illustrated in Figure 13.1, helps define problems more accurately. Use whatever format is most comfortable, but we urge you to analyze the problem in writing.

In the first section of your worksheet state as concisely as possible what the deviation or problem is.

The second section should help you structure a definition of your problem in terms of what the situation is, how this differs from the normal, and what is distinctive about the deviation. This should focus your attention on differences—usually in procedure—between what the problem is and what the problem is not. Of the four areas covered in this section, the first defines the actual deviation (or problem): What is it? The second helps you determine when the problem occurs. The third locates the problem—that is, where does it crop up? The fourth delimits the extent of the problem. All four of these areas should be carefully reexamined before proceeding further. To attempt to isolate a cause before defining the problem is unwise—and to propose a solution (even an interim solution) before understanding the cause(s) is also unwise.

Finally, the third section of the worksheet attempts to isolate some of the possible causes of the problem. These are tentative assertions only. If you have carefully followed the procedure to this point, your list of possible causes should be short—and it will probably be fairly accurate.

Select an interim solution

At this point, the biggest danger is leaping to a conclusion without thoroughly testing and retesting your thinking. It's easy to adopt one possible cause for a problem, then create arguments in its favor while rejecting any other possibilities.

Select an interim solution based on a review of your initial analysis of the problem. This prevents hasty choices and helps to refine the efforts you put into the Problem Analysis Worksheet.

But more important, it allows intelligent application of a managerial Band-Aid: Many problems require immediate attention. If a building is on fire, you put the fire out—then, once the immediate danger is past, you will want to determine why the fire started and institute measures to prevent a future fire.

One way to identify causes is to continually ask "What could cause this problem?" If you have three possible causes, A, B, and C, could the problem exist without one of these causes being operative? If you can eliminate a cause by showing that the problem can crop up without that particular cause in operation, then you have some grounds for rejecting that cause for that problem. If a proposed cause is always present when a problem occurs and is never present when that problem is not operant, then you have good grounds to think you have found the cause.

Usually, determining the cause of a problem will not be too difficult—but keep in mind that the most obvious cause may not be the correct underlying cause, and that an open mind plus some thought experiments may save a lot of effort later. (A thought experiment models the situation and lets you play with the variables one by one. It may be poor science, but it is often a good way to locate the roots of a problem.)

Once you are clear on the cause of a problem, two possibilities arise. First, you may have to apply an interim solution to keep your operation functioning smoothly. By knowing the cause—and keeping it in mind as you mull over possible stopgap solutions—your interim solution will probably be more effective than would otherwise be expected. A formal approach to this is presented in the next seven

Figure 13.1

Problem Analysis Worksheet

The following illustrates how problem solving can be applied to a typical problem: a cash flow slowdown. The techniques described in the rest of this chapter refer to the information contained in this example.

What is the problem?   Cash flow slowdown: Accounts Receivable (A/R) now average 55 days as opposed to 30 day maximum, a 25 day increase.

	The problem is:	*The problem is not:*	*The difference is:*
What	Drastic growth of large receivables: now 55 day average on accounts over $1,500 (some are repeat laggards)	Small accounts (under $1,000)	Small accounts pay up front and take discount; no single orders on credit
When	From November to now	Prior to November	Interest rate changes? Freer credit? Have we changed credit policy?
Where	N/A (no geographical difference—it's all over the country)		
Extent	70% of large accounts running up to 90+ days	30% of all large accounts, 30 day maximum, 90% small accounts	Some large accounts pay slowly, but others of the same volume pay in 30 days. (Could this be due to more personal contact with these customers?)

Possible Causes:
1. Looser credit policies. (Review please.)
2. Company is victim of cash management people. (Then what?)
3. Looser collection efforts. (Review please.)
4. Could be a tie-in with selling by mail—though repeaters are not mail customers.

steps. Second, whether an interim solution is needed or not, try to make sure that any solution adopted permanently is the best choice possible. Once the fire is out, don't forget to take great care to prevent further outbreaks. Test your interim solution (or non-solution) against other possible solutions.

Part Two:
What should be done about it?

The problem and its cause have been identified, and the crisis is over for the moment. Now what should be done?

The Chinese character for crisis has two parts, representing danger and opportunity respectively. Keep this in mind. The process covered in this part applies to opportunities as well as to choosing effective and permanent solutions to problems—and the dangers are that unless you choose wisely, the opportunity will slip away, the solution will be illusory, and the problem will recur (probably in a more intransigent form).

To apply the techniques to opportunities, begin by defining as in Part One—what standards or processes now operating will be affected? Why? Then proceed to set new objectives and examine ways to achieve them. This is a planning technique, and one that works pretty well.

Determine objectives of solution

These next seven steps are the trickiest part of the problem solving process. While considerable effort is called for in determining the cause of the problem, determining how best to solve that problem calls for managerial creativity.

Begin by determining the objectives you hope the solution will achieve. A problem—a deviation from a standard —will lead to a need for new standards. Suppose your problem is that sales are running three times over projections. A problem of this sort leads to setting up an entirely new set of objectives, ranging from reestablishing the old standard to setting newer, higher ones.

Objectives: To speed up collection of large institutional orders, to stop providing free (or almost free) financing to these accounts, and to improve cash flow. We need to get the biggest accounts to remain (or become) more profitable, cut financing costs, and reduce bank loans.

If you do not define what the objectives of a solution are, you can't tell if you have solved the problem, or are on the way to solving the problem, or if you are merely making the problem worse. Set down your objectives in writing. This will provide a sense of direction—plus some much needed feedback as to whether or not you are doing the right thing.

Classify objectives

One excellent way to split out the objectives so you can use them is to take a sheet of paper, draw a line down the middle, and head one column "Necessary" and the other "Desirable." Presumably all of the objectives which you've identified are desirable to a greater or lesser degree. Some of them will be vitally important. Put these in the "Necessary" column. These are the objectives which, if they are not met, prevent the solution from being satisfactory. Their satisfaction may even be necessary to the survival of your venture.

Other objectives are not necessary but merely desirable. Put such objectives in the "Desirable" column.

You may benefit by putting some time limits, however rough, on your objectives. For most purposes, make the objectives as specific as possible. This often requires added effort—but a specific objective will be more useful than a vague one.

Necessary

1. Improve collections: Reduce A/R age to 30 days.
2. Retain last year's margins.
3. Reduce dependence on short-term bank financing.
   (These goals to be achieved within 60 days.)
4. Maintain good relations with bulk customers.

Desirable

1. Improve margins 5 percent over last year's.
2. Reduce debt to X percent of sales.
3. Stop financing the slow-paying large accounts.
   (This can be done over 40 days—but aim for sooner.)

Develop alternative solutions

We would wager that few small business decisions are made based on a careful analysis of alternative possibilities. Unless you have more than one solution available, you cannot pick the best alternative—all you can do is ride with the one solution you have at hand.

Tentative list of alternatives:

1. Improve (and make more formal) collection efforts.
   Send reminder at 20 days, and call at 30 days. Keep
   on top of all accounts; better A/R management.
2. Restrict credit to fast-pay accounts.
3. Ask for 30 percent down, with order.
4. Increase discount, say to 5 percent /5N/10, 1.5 percent penalty after?
5. Do nothing. This is a temporary market aberration.

6. Sell more aggressively: You can still make money on late bulk due accounts and can finance receivables if necessary.
7. Maybe a combination of two or more of the above. Test?

Your alternatives should be picked with your objectives in mind. The interim solution is first aid, an attack on the symptoms rather than on the disease—but in order to permanently solve the problem, a more careful solution may be needed.

You may find that the interim solution is the permanent solution. Fine—just make sure it is the best choice—and remember that choice presupposes variety.

Compare alternatives with ordered objectives

In order to choose the best solution to the problem, you have to compare alternative solutions with the objectives. This will give you a fairly accurate idea of what solution is the best—all things being equal.

This may be made as mathematical as you wish. You can weight your decision or you may choose to follow a simpler method. For most decisions, a qualitative approach will produce adequate results. If you are happier with a quantitative approach, then a weighted method may appeal to you more. Both approaches force a comparison of alternatives with the desired objectives.

The important part of this step is to rank alternatives in order of their probability of achieving your objectives.

Choose a tentative solution

Which proposed solution, prima facie, most nearly meets the desired objectives? To even be considered as a solution, an alternative has to fit all of the "necessary" requirements and, ordinarily, a solution which has all of the "necessaries" and most of the "desirables"—or more of the "desirables" than any other solution—will be your first choice.

Careful attention to satisfying the "necessaries" prevents serious problems. It is all too easy to make decisions on the basis of the "desirables" column and ignore one of the "necessary" items.

For example, on the Tentative List of Alternatives above, alternatives two and five were eliminated at this point. The second alternative would alienate some customers, and repeat orders are critical. Alternative five would ignore the problem and erode working capital. On the other hand, alternatives three and four together looked promising, while alternative one could be immediately applied. (That is, alternative seven seems like the best choice.)

Assess adverse possibilities and consequences

You may find that one of the solutions is so dominant that all other alternatives fade into the background.

Even so, it is advisable at this point, before implementing the proposed solution, to try to assess its possible adverse consequences.

A solution can foreshadow possible difficulties, particularly in a business where clearly defined goals have been established and where well-defined processes and procedures have been practiced. Consider the people it will affect, the resources it will require, and the opportunities it may prevent.

But once again, there is no step-by-step procedure which you can follow to ensure that you make foresighted decisions. The best you can do is to try to think through the effects of implementing a solution before committing yourself.

In the A/R example solution, it was found that alternative one took time, but less time than originally thought. Alternative three scared off some accounts; this had to be modified on a case basis, not implemented across the board. The fourth alternative was too expensive—staying with 2/10, N30 terms, but absorbing freight on fast payments proved best. Alternative six, selling more aggressively, had to be shelved: More sales would aggravate the A/R problem, unless commitment to fast payment could be established.

Control adverse consequences; reassess alternatives if necessary

You may find after assessing the consequences of your decision that a solution which appeared most desirable has possible consequences you cannot live with. In this case, reassess the available alternatives. Do not forget that living with a problem can be an acceptable alternative, particularly if the consequences of all the other alternatives are worse than the problem itself.

A more likely situation is that you will have a very limited number of alternatives which satisfy your requirements. You may find that the one which appeared strongest at first glance has consequences you are unwilling to accept, while a less obvious solution has fewer or perhaps no unacceptable consequences.

This is not an easy step. All solutions have a few adverse consequences—but most will be manageable. If you don't foresee them, though, all you will do is create a new set of problems—which (compounded by taking you off guard) can be worse than the original problem. If you can control the adverse consequences by altering your plans or by careful preplanning, then you may find that what appeared at first glance to be an unacceptable solution will actually be the most desirable.

Action Plan For:
"An Approach to Problem Solving"

❏ Determine how much your problem deviates from your standards.

❏ Define your problem in terms of where and when it occurs and what its extent is.

❏ Select an interim solution based on your initial analysis.

❏ Focus on the objectives the solution will achieve, and classify them according to whether they're "necessary" or "desirable."

❏ Make a list of alternative solutions and compare them to your objectives.

❏ Choose a tentative solution from your list.

❏ Carefully assess the consequences of your solution.

❏ Control the adverse consequences by altering your plans or by reassessing your alternatives if necessary.

Chapter Fourteen:

Public Relations

....

One way to avoid certain problems is by having a carefully planned public relations program. But public relations can do a lot more than that—it can also increase your firm's sales without forcing you to spend a lot on advertising.

Public relations works as a "hidden persuader." The messages you want your prospects to receive are communicated in an "editorial" way.

Public relations works because people trust articles and news features more than they trust "advertising." People approach advertising from a skeptical point of view. Advertising is "selling," and nobody likes to be "sold." But articles and non-selling features are approached from an open-minded, "learning" point of view. As a result, public relations can do things that advertising can't do, at far less cost.

What is public relations?

Public relations can be defined as "non-advertising media activities which increase your firm's profitability." This involves everything from sending simple press releases to creating special programs designed to capture your market's imagination. Typical activities include:

- Articles favorably describing your firm's financial performance
- Articles featuring your firm's products or services, and how customers use them
- Calendar listings of special events involving your firm

- New product previews
- Interviews
- Sponsoring local events, like marathons
- Speaking or participating in panel discussions at trade shows or conferences

It's important to emphasize how often what we read as "news" actually originates in a firm's public relations department. A study by the *Columbia Journalism Review* showed that 111 of the stories featured on the inside pages of an issue of the *Wall Street Journal* originated as press releases! In 70 percent of the cases, in fact, the articles were run as received, without adding additional information.*

* Alan Caruba, "Public Relations: What is it?" *New Jersey Business*, November 1982, page 70. Quoted in Bob Bly's *The Copywriter's Handbook* (see "Suggestions for Further Reading").

Bly, Robert W. *The Copywriter's Handbook: A step-by-step guide to writing copy that sells* (New York: Dodd, Mead & Company, 1985). $17.95 hardcover. Chapter 9, "Writing Public Relations Material," contains many useful ideas, sample press release formats, and answers to frequently asked questions.

To understand how public relations can convert prospects into customers at a relatively low cost, consider the following three case studies:

Case Study Number One: "The Concorde Is Coming!"

Problem:

A Pacific Northwest restaurant wanted to differentiate itself from its competition by emphasizing its extensive selection of the latest imported wines.

Solution:

The restaurant arranged for a grand tour of European vineyards, returning to Seattle from France on the supersonic Concorde with a shipment of wines the same day the latest French wines were released.

Results:

The charter was the Concorde's first visit to Seattle. The Concorde arrived late afternoon at the city's in-town airport. While in Seattle, the Concorde was on display, and flew one-hour charters over the Pacific. All proceeds were donated to a local charity.

The promotion received tremendous preevent and post event newspaper and television coverage. Numerous articles and columns were written about it, and photographs of the Concorde's visit were on the front pages of both daily newspapers. Local television covered the Concorde's landing and interviewed tour members. The restaurant's name was on everyone's tongue in this aviation-oriented town (where Boeing has its home).

No amount of advertising could have accomplished the exposure and positioning the restaurant received. For less than the cost of a series of magazine and newspaper ads, the restaurant became a celebrity in itself, respected for both its wine and its community orientation.

Case Study Number Two: Building Credibility Through Articles

Problem:

The ex-advertising manager of a four-store retail chain wanted to leverage his local success into a nationwide business. An unknown outside his own community, he needed to quickly generate national exposure and credibility.

Solution:

The answer was a series of monthly advertising articles in the industry's leading trade magazine.

Results:

His articles gave the previously unknown writer "instant expert" status and established client confidence in his abilities. His warm and friendly writing style helped retailers view him as "one of them," rather than as an "outsider." Four months into the article series, he was selling catalogue formats for $1,000 to retailers he had never met.

The article series generated business and eliminated the need for advertising. And he was paid for writing the articles.

Case Study Number Three: Becoming the "Safe" Place to Buy

Problem:

How do you differentiate yourself from the competition when you're selling the products other stores are selling at the same—or lower—prices?

Solution:

The answer is to adopt the "Safe Buy" position. This generates buyer confidence before customers even enter your store.

Results:

An enterprising audio/video retailer in the competitive Providence, Rhode Island, market achieved this by arranging for one of the industry's most respected journalists to visit his store and present a non-selling demonstration of the latest digital audio technology.

The event was planned far in advance, and local media were informed well in advance of the journalist's visit. Preevent publicity stressed the journalist's independence and the educational purpose of the demonstration.

The store was packed the day of the presentation. Most important, the television news team showed up to film the presentation and interview the owner and members of the audience. They were so impressed, they returned to film a series on changing audio/video technology, narrated by the store owner. Installments were run on the 6:00 p.m. evening news.

This exposure generated immediate sales and established the store's credibility. Equally important, the store owner became the informal spokesman for the consumer electronics industry in his town. Business editors and other newsmen got in the habit of calling him whenever they had a question on either audio/video technology or retailing conditions.

What do these examples of public relations programs have in common?

1. *In each case, the firm knew exactly what it wanted to accomplish.* Each firm could reduce the purpose of its public relations program to a simple statement.

- The Seattle restaurant wanted to become known for its extensive selection of imported wines.
- The ex-advertising manager wanted to establish nationwide credibility.
- The Providence audio/video retailer wanted to become the "safe" place to buy.

2. *Each firm was able to identify the target market it wanted to influence.* Furthermore, each firm understood its target market's needs.

- The Seattle restaurant knew that it was selling "excitement" as well as wine to high-income, status-conscious consumers.
- The ex-advertising manager understood that sales would follow confidence.
- The Rhode Island retailer knew that most customers were confused about consumer electronics and were willing to pay extra for the security of knowing they were making the right choice.

3. *Each firm knew how to structure its message in terms the media could easily deal with.* This is probably the most important point. Millions of press releases are sent out each year, but only a few are printed. This is because most press releases lack "news" or "information" value. Editors are swamped with press

releases which are of little or no value to anyone other than the firm sending them out. These "brag and boast" press releases are immediately discarded.

To succeed, your public relations activities must have news or information value.

- The Seattle restaurant received widespread front-page and prime-time press coverage because:
a. It was the first visit of the Concorde to Seattle (news value).
b. There is genuine excitement in the idea of new French wines received in Seattle the same day they are released in France.
c. Proceeds went to charity. Thus, the media weren't merely supporting a local business's public relations efforts; the media's efforts would also help a favorite local charity.
- The ex-advertising manager's public relations campaign received media support because:
a. The articles were of genuine value. The articles strengthened the magazine's editorial content, which translates into higher readership and higher advertising rates.
b. The articles were sent in finished form, with illustrations and artwork. They were carefully edited and proofread before they were sent. This made the editor happy, as it saved tremendous amounts of time.
- The Providence retailer capitalized on the local media's desire to build up the local businesses. This strengthens the local economy, meaning additional revenue opportunities.

Satisfy both markets

To meet your firm's communications objectives, two markets must be satisfied. You need to satisfy both the media and the target market's needs. This is in contrast to advertising, where you can be certain your message will run because the media is paid to run it.

First you have to convince the media that your communication has definite news value. Editors and television reporters are not interested in running free ads for you. Their integrity demands that their articles and news features contain information which will truly benefit their readers or viewers.

Second, your target market has to be convinced it will benefit from reading or viewing your communication. Readers and viewers are only interested in your message to the extent that it offers them a benefit. Your message has to be stated in genuine newsworthy terms. Your target market has to learn something which relates to them, helping them solve problems or satisfy preexisting needs.

Active versus passive public relations

Public relations can be active or passive.

Active programs are those which attempt to change existing attitudes. These programs predispose customers to be more receptive to your advertising and sales presentations.

Active programs begin with a description of current customer belief as well as a statement of the beliefs you want your prospects to have. Active public relations programs are long-term, goal-oriented programs which fit into the firm's overall corporate communications program.

Passive public relations programs are short-term and defensive in nature. They are designed to offset bad publicity or eliminate environmental threats (e.g., proposed governmental regulations). Often, they attempt to divert media or public interest from a negative aspect of a firm to a more positive aspect (e.g., stressing a toxic waste dump's economic contribution to the community).

Both active and passive programs have their place, although most firms gain more benefits from "positive" programs.

Establishing your own public relations program

Planning and analysis is the first step in putting together a successful public relations program. You need to define the existing state of affairs. You have to get inside your prospects' minds so you can prepare a detailed Situation Analysis.

In your Situation Analysis, you want to answer questions like:

- What do people think of us now?
- What position do we occupy in our prospects' minds?
- What concerns do buyers have when they go shopping for our product or service?

Next you'll want to put together an Action Plan. Your Action Plan will define the goals of your program and outline the steps necessary to achieve them.

Your Action Plan should include answers to questions like:

- How do we want our prospects to view our business?
- How should we be positioned in the prospects' minds?
- What will motivate them to take action?

Other questions to be answered at this point include:

- Who are the influencers, and how can we get them to carry our message to our prospects?
- What's the time frame of our activities—what will happen when? Who has responsibility for doing it?

- How do these activities relate to other aspects of our marketing mix, like advertising and sales promotion?

Execution and follow-up come next. Execution is often the easiest stage of all, since the goals and schedule have already been established. Execution involves teamwork, delegation, and attention to detail. The execution phase is often more pleasurable, because it involves action and offers creative opportunities which allow one's imagination to flourish.

Follow-up involves evaluating the success of your program and making the most of your gains. Evaluation is crucial, so you can build on your successes and avoid the mistakes of the past.

Process versus event

Perhaps the most important element in a successful public relations program is to view it as an ongoing process, not an isolated event.

Sophisticated public relations campaigns involve a series of projects which overlap each other. Some projects may be in the planning phase while others are in the execution stage, and others are in the follow-up stage.

All projects, however, work toward agreed-upon program goals.

Public relations involves more than simply sending out press releases highlighting recent company promotions. Public relations involves a wide variety of activities—from surveys and attitude studies to article writing, arranging European charters, supporting local charities, and taking part in community events.

Thus, public relations often consists of "creating news." It involves deciding what the media considers news and then creating an event which will qualify as news—even though it furthers the firm's objectives.

In the first case study, for example, the Concorde's first landing at Boeing Field qualified as news, even

---

Figure 14.1

Cost Advantages

Compare the cost of a public relations campaign with traditional advertising methods:

Cost of printing 100 2-page press releases:	$20.00
Postage to mail 100 press releases:	25.00
Envelopes:	5.00
Total:	$50.00

Consider: How many column inches of advertising does $50.00 buy in your local newspaper? How many minutes of radio or television advertising does $50.00 buy? In most cases, a $50.00 media investment would be easily ignored. But $50.00 spent sending the right press release to the right people can result in thousands of dollars' worth of favorable editorial support.

A well-planned public relations program can reach more people at lower cost than any advertising media. Just be sure your press release has news value.

though the resulting news stories publicized the restaurant's extensive selection of imported wines.

In the second case study, the ex-advertising manager's "How to Advertise" articles satisfied the trade magazine's desire to help retailers advertise more effectively, even though the articles helped the writer achieve nationwide prominence.

In the third case study, the television news reporter's primary goal was to acquaint viewers with the latest audio/video technology, even though it gave the participating retailer an advantage over his competition.

Six steps toward a successful public relations program

1. Decide on the purpose of your public relations program.

What message are you trying to communicate? What attitude are you trying to change? What action have you taken?

2. Identify your target market and become familiar with their needs.

Who are you trying to influence? What are their needs? What influences their behavior? What are their concerns?

3. Identify the "influencers" and become familiar with their needs.

Which medium is best suited for communicating your message? Who decides what features are published or broadcast? What criteria do they use in deciding what to feature in their articles or broadcasts?

4. Make it easy for everyone concerned.

This usually involves communicating your message as quickly and simply as possible. Your press materials should clearly and concisely communicate all necessary information, including sources of additional information. Photographs should be clearly identified. Making it easy involves working as far ahead as possible. This makes it easy for influencers to fit your program into their schedule.

5. Get assistance where necessary.

Professional assistance can mean the difference between success and failure. Outside public relations professionals can help you plan and smoothly execute your program, as well as help you avoid problems you might not expect.

6. Follow up on your program.

Make the most of your public relations successes. Send colleagues and prospects reprints of favorable articles that have featured your business. Maintain a scrapbook of press clippings in your waiting room. Framed copies of articles and favorable product reviews also help keep your success alive.

Most important, learn to say thank you when an editor or publication has presented your firm in a favorable light. This person-to-person ambassadorship can pay big dividends in the months ahead. People naturally tend to want to do business again with people who have been nice to them in the past.

Figure 14.2

Simple Self-analysis

When evaluating present or proposed public relations activities, ask yourself "So what?"

If you cannot answer the question in a positive way which relates to the media's and your market's dual self-interest, your public relations campaign is likely to fail.

Example:

A press release describing your firm's intra-league bowling scores is unlikely to be of interest to anyone other than team members. A press release describing how your bowling team's Year-End Tournament raised $5,000 for a local hospital is more likely to run.

But, a press release showing the president presenting your check to the local charity will definitely run.

Questions to ask when shopping for a public relations agency

The best way to select the right public relations agency is to conduct an agency search. Visit several agencies to get their feel. Then invite the three or four best contenders to your office for a serious presentation.

Submit the following questions in writing, and ask the finalists to address them in their presentation. By asking agencies to focus on the same issues, you'll gain a better idea of how the agencies differ from one another.

What process does your agency use in analyzing client needs? Describe in detail.

A successful public relations program involves planning as much as execution. You'll want to convince yourself that the agency has the "mental horsepower" necessary to see beyond the obvious and move your public relations program beyond the limits of your own abilities.

Once client needs have been determined, what is the process used to position a company?

You'll want to be convinced that the agency is capable of developing a creative strategy for your firm. You want to make sure the agency understands the strengths and limitations of positioning. What process will they use in developing your firm's communications goals?

How does the agency measure how effectively it's achieving its client's goals?

You'll want to be convinced that the agency will work with you in developing meaningful standards for measuring the success of your public relations program. Results can be measured in attitude changes, exposure, or revenue dollars created.

What reporting procedures do you use in keeping the client informed about your activities?

Many agency/client relationships founder on this issue. Successful agencies operate on a "no surprise" basis, keeping clients informed about program development, media contacts, and costs incurred. These agencies spell out in advance exactly how much their services will cost.

Describe your agency's experience working with firms like us. What success stories can you point to in our field? Whom may we contact?

You'll probably be most comfortable working with a public relations agency with experience in your particular field. Equally important, you'll want to deal with an agency which is comfortable working with a firm of your size.

Describe your agency's media relationships. Are you on a first-name basis with important influencers in our field?

Public relations agencies are at an advantage when they can pick up a phone and talk directly to an important editor or columnist. A single phone call can assure that a press release is plucked from the bottom of the pile and brought to the top for immediate attention.

Describe a successful program you have been involved with for a client similar to our firm. What were the goals of the program? What strategies and tactics were used? How did you measure your success?

Your goal is to separate "fact" from "selling." You're searching for solid evidence that the agency can do what it promises, by pointing to evidence from the past.

Describe your agency's approach to creativity. How do you measure creativity? How do you involve your clients in the creative process?

The agency's response to these questions will help you decide how focused and disciplined the agency is. You want to be convinced that the agency views creativity as a tool, not an end in itself.

The day of your agency review, ask the following questions. These will test your agency's integrity and ability to perform under pressure.

How strongly do you stand up for what you believe? What do you do if a client insists you do something you feel is against their best interests?

The agency's response to this question will help you determine the agency's integrity level and help you ascertain how challenging the agency relationship is likely to be. It will help you avoid hiring "yes men" who will simply perpetuate your limitations.

What important clients have you lost during the past year? Why did you lose them? May we contact them?

Another "stunner," this question will help you determine the ethical stability of the agency. An agency that badmouths a previous client is likely to badmouth you, too, in the future.

The most important question of all...

Who will be actually working on our account on a day-to-day basis?

Many times, clients find that the only time they see top-level agency management is during agency reviews.

It's important to make sure that the people who sell you the agency's services are the same people you'll be working with on a day-to-day basis.

Action Plan For:
"Public Relations"

❏ Determine the purpose of your public relations program. What will your message be, in one sentence?

❏ Identify your target market and the influences, and become familiar with their needs.

❏ Make sure your communication has definite news value for the media and benefits for the readers or viewers.

❏ Communicate your message clearly and professionally. Make yourself easy to work with.

❏ Get help from an agency if you need it, and evaluate the services of several before you make a commitment to using one.

❏ Follow up and evaluate the success of your program.

Resources for
Small Businesses

....

There are many excellent texts available on small business management, but most are more appropriate for businesses with more than 100 employees. Check out your local library, college bookstores and these sources of small business management information:

Upstart Publishing Company, Inc. These publications on proven management techniques for small businesses are available from Upstart Publishing Company, Inc., 12 Portland Street, Dover, NH 03820. For a free current catalogue, call 800-235-8866 outside New Hampshire or 749-5071 in state.

- **Managing by the Numbers: Financial Essentials for the Growing Business**, © 1992, David H. Bangs, Jr. and Upstart Publishing Company, Inc. This book makes financial management simple for the small business owner. It provides straightforward techniques for getting maximum return with a minimum of detail. Includes anecdotes, examples, case histories, forms and worksheets. (Softcover, 150 pages, $19.95)

- **The Start Up Guide: A One-Year Plan for Entrepreneurs**, © 1989, David H. Bangs, Jr. and Upstart Publishing Company, Inc. This book utilizes the same step-by-step, no-jargon method as the Business Planning Guide to assist those with no formal training through the process of beginning a successful business. (Softcover, 150 pages, $18.95)

- **On Your Own: A Woman's Guide to Building a Business**, © 1990, Laurie Zuckerman and Upstart Publishing Company, Inc. **On Your Own** is for women who want hands-on, practical information about starting and running a business. It deals honestly with issues like finding time for your business when you're also the primary care provider, societal biases against women and credit discrimination. (Softcover, 224 pages, $18.95)

- **Buy the Right Business—At the Right Price,** © 1990, Brian Knight and the Associates of Country Business, Inc. and Upstart Publishing Company, Inc. Many people who would like to be in business for themselves think strictly of starting a business. In some cases, buying a going concern may be preferable—and just as affordable. (Softcover, 150 pages, $18.95)

- **Market Planning Guide,** © 1987, 1989, 1990, David H. Bangs, Jr. and Upstart Publishing Company, Inc. A 150-page manual to help small-business owners put together a goal-oriented, resource-based marketing plan with action steps, benchmarks and timelines. Includes worksheets and checklists to make implementation and review easier. (Softcover, 150 pages, $18.95)

- **Cash Flow Control Guide,** © 1987, 1990, David H. Bangs, Jr. and Upstart Publishing Company, Inc. A manual to help small-business owners solve their number-one financial problem. Includes worksheets and checklists. (Softcover, 70 pages, $10.95)

- **Personnel Planning Guide,** © 1986, 1987, 1988, 1990, David H. Bangs, Jr. and Upstart Publishing Company, Inc. A 160-page manual outlining practical and proven personnel management techniques, including hiring, managing, evaluating and compensating personnel. Includes worksheets and checklists. (Softcover, 160 pages, $18.95)

- **The Business Planning Guide,** © 1976, 1985, 1989, 1990, David H. Bangs, Jr. and Upstart Publishing Company, Inc. A 150-page manual that helps you write a business plan and financing proposal tailored to your business, your goals and your resources. Includes worksheets and checklists. (Softcover, 150 pages, $18.95)

Small Business Reporter. An excellent series of booklets on small-business management published by Bank of America, Department 3120, PO Box 37000, San Francisco, CA 94137; (415) 622-2491. Individual copies are $5 each. Ask for a list of current titles—they have about 17 available, including Steps to Starting a Business, Avoiding Management Pitfalls, Business Financing and Marketing Small Business.

In Business. A bimonthly magazine for small businesses, especially those with less than 10 employees. The publisher is J.G. Press, PO Box 323, Emmaus, PA 18049. Annual subscriptions are $18.

The Great Brain Robbery, Ray Considine and Murray Raphel, © 1980, 1981, by The Great Brain Robbery, 1360 East Rubio Street, Altadena, CA 91101. Subtitled "A collection of proven ideas to make you money and change your life!", **The Great Brain Robbery** contains numerous checklists and ideas which are thought-provoking. The chapters entitled "Formula for Success," "Secret Selling Sentences," and "If You Don't Like It Here, Get Out!" are particularly provocative. Raphel and Considine are marketing and promotional experts—which is apparent throughout this book.

Marketing with Facts, © 1986, published by Price Waterhouse, 1251 Avenue of the Americas, New York, NY 10020. This book, part of a series aimed at small-business owners and entrepreneurs, focuses on how marketing information can be used to enhance opportunities for profit. The book's lists of questions and lexicon of marketing terminology are particularly helpful. Copies of this book cost $5.00 and are available at any Price Waterhouse office.

Additional Resources

....

Small Business Development Centers (SBDCs). Call your state university or the Small Business Administration (SBA) to find the SBDC nearest you. Far and away the best free management program available, SBDCs provide expert assistance and training in every aspect of business management. Don't ignore this resource.

SCORE, or Service Corps of Retired Executives, sponsored by the U.S. Small Business Administration, provides free counseling and also a series of workshops and seminars for small businesses. Of special interest: SCORE offers a Business Planning Workshop which includes a 30-minute video produced specifically for SCORE by Upstart Publishing and funded by Paychex, Inc. There are over 500 SCORE chapters nationwide. For more information, contact the SBA office nearest you and ask about SCORE.

Small Business Administration (SBA). The SBA offers a number of management assistance programs. If you are assigned a capable Management Assistance Officer, you have an excellent resource. The SBA is worth a visit, if only to leaf through their extensive literature.

Colleges and universities. Most have business courses. Some have SBDCs, others have more specialized programs. Some have small-business expertise—the University of New Hampshire, for example, has two schools which provide direct small-business management assistance.

Keye Productivity Center, P.O. Box 23192, Kansas City, MO 64141. Keye Productivity offers business seminars on specific personnel topics for a reasonable fee. Call them at 800-821-3919 for topics and prices. Their seminar entitled

Hiring and Firing is excellent, well-documented and useful. Good handout materials are included.

Comprehensive Accounting Corporation, 2111 Comprehensive Drive, Aurora, IL 60507. CAC has over 425 franchised offices providing accounting, bookkeeping and management consulting services to small businesses. For information, call 800-323-9009.

Center for Entrepreneurial Management, 29 Greene Street, New York, NY 10013. The oldest and largest nonprofit membership association for small-business owners in the world. They maintain an extensive list of books, videotapes, cassettes and other small-business management aids. Call 212-925-7304 for information.

Libraries. Do not forget to take advantage of the information readily available at your library.

Index